BE YOUR
BEST

T0048477

SMARTER SHARPER THINKING

**Reduce Stress, Banish
Fatigue and Find Focus**

JENNY BROCKIS

WILEY

First published as *Future Brain* in 2016 by John Wiley & Sons Australia, Ltd
42 McDougall St, Milton Qld 4064

Office also in Melbourne

This edition first published in 2019 by John Wiley & Sons Australia, Ltd

Typeset in 12.5/14.5pt Arno Pro

© Rossvale Holdings Pty Ltd ATF The Brockis Family Trust t/a Brain Fit 2016

The moral rights of the author have been asserted

Cover design by Wiley

Internal figures designed by Kate Matheson

Printed in United States of America by Quad/Graphics

V224499_022619

Disclaimer
The material in this publication is of the nature of general comment only, and does not represent professional advice. It is not intended to provide specific guidance for particular circumstances and it should not be relied on as the basis for any decision to take action or not take action on any matter which it covers. Readers should obtain professional advice where appropriate, before making any such decision. To the maximum extent permitted by law, the author and publisher disclaim all responsibility and liability to any person, arising directly or indirectly from any person taking or not taking action based on the information in this publication.

To Tom and Sophie, you are the future.

First we managed time, then we managed attention, now it's all about performance. In *Smarter Sharper Thinking* Dr Brockis is tackling possibly the single most important factor in high performance — the hardware in our skull. Ranging from workflow issues to lifestyle issues to physiological hacks for optimising our organic super computer, this book is jam-packed with well-researched and highly practical tips and strategies.

Matt Church, CEO and founder of Thought Leaders Global and author of *Amplifiers*

This book is a practical roadmap for a healthy, alert and adaptive brain. If we keep our brain healthy, everything else will take care of itself.

Graeme Cowan, leadership and resilience speaker and author of *Thriving Naturally*

Smarter Sharper Thinking is an essential read for any leader that wants to ensure they continue to lead into the future with relevance and competitive advantage. Dr Brockis shares her expertise, advice and essential must-dos to adapt and change for higher performance: to lead yourself, your team and your business, and ensure your continued success.

Janine Garner, speaker, best-selling author, and CEO of LBDG

Dr Jenny Brockis has taken the latest findings in neuroscience and distilled them into a readable, actionable 12-step plan to improve brain health, mental performance, resilience and happiness in the workplace. Dr Brockis deftly explains that high-performance thinking is not hard, but it does require us to look after our brain in the right way. Essential reading for every employer and employee.

Dr Sarah McKay, neuroscientist and science writer

Dr Jenny Brockis lights up the world with her much-needed work on how we can all future-proof our brains. Jenny makes complex neuroscientific messages accessible and practical with her warmth, wit and smarts. An award-winning communicator, Jenny helps business leaders, managers and educators get better results in everything they do, by simply using their brains better.

Yamini Naidu, business storyteller, best-selling author, speaker and mentor

Contents

About the author

Dr Jenny Brockis is a medical practitioner, healthy brain advocate and future mind planner. She is the Director and founder of Brain Fit and author of two previous books, *Brain Fit!* and *Brain Smart*.

A self-confessed nerd, Jenny is a lifelong learner. She graduated as a Nightingale Nurse (St. Thomas' Hospital London), then as a doctor (MB ChB Bristol), FRACGP, with further postgraduate qualifications in Lifestyle Medicine, Nutritional and Environmental Medicine, the Neuroscience of Leadership, and has undertaken training in Mindfulness Meditation.

Jenny is an expert in brain fitness, which she defines as what it takes for individuals and organisations to stay brain healthy, eliminate poor thinking skills and boost mental performance. Her goal is to make brain fitness as well known and understood as Jamie Oliver has made healthy eating.

Passionate, eloquent and inspiring, Jenny's keynotes and workshops provide cutting-edge insights into how neuroscience provides the perfect pathway to navigate our complex, complicated and busy world. Never content simply to go with the status quo, Jenny is dedicated to her quest to promote the development of a brain-friendly culture that nurtures and develops all brains at work.

When not speaking, writing or researching, Jenny enjoys spending time with her husband and two young adult children, travelling the world and challenging her longstanding fear of heights.

Acknowledgements

Like crafting an Oscar acceptance speech, writing the acknowledgments for this book has been almost harder than writing the book itself, because there are so many people to thank. Each deserves their own special recognition for their contribution, for which I am forever deeply grateful.

This book would never have seen the light of day without the input, advice and wisdom that only a magnificent mentor can provide. Matt Church, it was tough love on occasions, but you provided what was needed to lift, nurture and develop my ideas. Thank you for always expecting more, for raising the bar, and getting me to do the work.

Tiffany Turpin, your editing ability to help turn what was originally a complete dog's breakfast into a decent first draft was much appreciated.

To the Wiley team, Chris, Ingrid and Peter, thank you so much for your support and guidance throughout the process. To Lucy Raymond an especial thank you for your initial belief in this book, that allowed the dream to become a reality.

Jem Bates, thank you so much for making the editing process such a constructive and enjoyable process. Your ability to sharpen up my writing and condense ideas into a more reader-friendly format has been invaluable.

Kate Matheson, thank you for all your input into the book and the great design work for the graphics.

Then there are all those supporters in the stands, the people who have contributed both directly or indirectly to the birth of this book. To my fellow speakers and world class presenters on our Showcase journey in 2014: Yamini Naidu, Janine Garner, Lynne Cazaly, Angela Lockwood, Jamie Pride, Natasha Pincus and Marcus Bird — thank you. To Janine, who never failed to remind me that a Yorkshire lass never leaves the house without her big girl's pants on. To my fellow thought leaders Jason Fox, Gihan Perera and Mike House — thank you. You all continue to inspire me in my quest to share my message around the planet.

Cath Sutherland and Claire Savage, your friendship, support, fireside chats and raw chocolate treats have meant so much.

The one person without whom I would never have started this new journey and transformation from GP to professional speaker and author is my wonderful husband John, who has always believed in what I do and provided unconditional love and support; from always being there to pick me up from yet another late night flight back into Perth, to quietly just getting on with cooking dinner and sorting out all the other things going on at home, when he knows my 'I'm just finishing this' means I'll be more than a little while longer working in the back office.

To Tom and Sophie, who have grown into such beautiful, strong, well-rounded individuals. I'm so proud of everything you do and the people you have become. I love you to bits. This book is for you.

And finally thank you to you, the reader, for taking the time to stop and read this book, and discover what you can use to create your own high-performance brain.

Preface

We talk a lot as business leaders about the need for adaptability and innovative practices. This makes perfect sense, because we are living in a time of unparalleled change. Information, technology, the way we produce things — it's all on the fast track. We need to be able to match the pace of innovation.

What I find interesting is that nobody ever really discusses how we are going to achieve this. Yes, we can educate ourselves. Yes, we can do research and keep up with digital technology as it changes. But what about our ability to increase our mental flexibility, agility and adaptability?

HOW ARE WE ACTUALLY GOING TO MAKE OUR BRAINS PERFORM BETTER AND AT A HIGHER LEVEL SO WE CAN TAKE IN ALL OF THIS CHANGE?

This is about more than survival; it's about evolution.

In the age of information and innovation, the currency of knowledge is necessarily being replaced by our ability to think — and to think as well as we possibly can. We can initiate this change through greater brain awareness. For this we need to understand what is required to create and operate a thriving brain.

Smarter Sharper Thinking reveals how you can use the latest discoveries from the brain science for your brain's advantage. It also sets out to answer some of the questions around how to build a brain for the future.

What will the future brain look like? Read on. You'll be surprised at what you find.

Introduction

The current work environment is not a happy place in the main. Increasing levels of stress and anxiety, perceptions of time poverty and change fatigue, the effects of chronic medical conditions and depression on workflow — business is not booming. In *Future Brain* we examine these very big areas of concern and discuss how strategies based on neuroscientific research can be used to reduce their impact by offering practical solutions for individuals and organisations.

Back to the future brain

Our brain has received a bad rap for far too long. If you think of it in social media terms, our brain is a community page with about 300 likes. Why? Largely because, until fairly recently, we have been remarkably ignorant of the workings of our own minds.

Now, however, we have access to brilliant studies from neurologists, neuroscientists, psychiatrists and other researchers who are delving into why our brain works the way it does, and why we need to keep it as fit as we possibly can.

It is this research that has led to the development of the 12 Keys of *Smarter Sharper Thinking*, which break down the academispeak to provide understandable, easy-to-implement ways for all of us to become better thinkers.

Working nine to five. And six to twelve. And ...

The standard working week is now almost as extinct as the dinosaurs. The distinction between work and home time is becoming ever more blurred. Perceptions of how we do our work, where we do it and even why we do it are shifting.

Flexibility of work hours may mean our working in several jobs or a change in the location of where we are expected to or allowed to do our work. Increasing globalisation means we are constantly interacting with overseas marketplaces, which has led to the concept of being 'open all hours'. Our brains are, as a result, exhausted.

With greater technological capabilities than ever before, and with medical research at its peak, will we find a magic pill or potion to enable us to develop brain superpowers? Will there be a cerebral update chip that our health/brain practitioner can install when we attend our regular brain check-ups?

Or is there another solution, such as choosing to manage and use our brain better? Could it really be as simple as that?

If we dismiss the basics, we miss the point.

When I worked in general practice, my clients came to see me because they were sick. After all, that was my job: to make a diagnosis and provide a treatment to allow the patient to recover. But much of the time their sickness was a consequence of poor health and lifestyle choices. Not from ignorance, but just from trying to keep up with everything in their daily lives.

I also noticed that one environment that contributes heavily to the burden of disease, injury and mental distress is the one we call *work*. The modern workplace is very often a source of visible and non-visible harm, a toxic and unwieldy monster. The challenge before us is to address the stark reality that this is not only doing us physical harm but is costing us dearly in many aspects of our lives.

Depression is now the second leading cause of workplace disability globally. Type 2 diabetes is the fastest growing chronic condition in Australia. According to *Sick at Work*, a research paper published by Medibank in 2011, the total cost of *presenteeism* was reported as $AUD34.1 billion for 2009–10, equivalent to a loss of 2.7 per cent of GDP and has remained at this level in 2016. Presenteeism is the loss of productivity that occurs when an employee turns up for work but works at a lower capacity than normal because of illness, stress or other distractions. Presenteeism costs the Australian economy more than absenteeism, which itself in 2017 was estimated at $AUD44 billion, with a direct cost of $578 per employee per day.

While the research clearly indicates the problem is huge, the implication is also that this problem is not going to go away any time soon, and indeed is likely to increase.

It is also possible that these figures underestimate the reality. Every one of us is impacted by different life events, concerns and worries at any given time. We might be super-productive, highly organised and excellent at our job, but we all have those times when we will be 'off' due to minor health ailments, family worries or extra-stressful circumstances at work.

Absenteeism is fairly easily defined in terms of specific time off for reasons of ill-health or injury. Presenteeism, though, is a far harder animal to corral.

It's time for greater organisational health

From an individual perspective, when we speak of keeping fit and healthy, we are really talking about taking care of our minds and bodies so we can do what we want, when we want and as we want. The relatively recent concept of *brain health* signifies far more than simply a new term for mental health and wellbeing.

Brain health is about creating a fit and healthy brain that is then optimised to operate at its best, and a big part of that happens in our work life.

In the workplace, organisational health is about ensuring the complete health, safety and wellbeing of all who work there. The focus of OHS has traditionally been on preventing physical injury; what is needed now is the integration of brain and mind health into this model.

Bill Withers, founder of acQuire Technology Solutions, speaking at a conference I attended a couple of years ago, gave a nice analogy on the need to view a business (of any size) as a living organism. Just as a human being comprises trillions of living cells, a business is also the sum of its parts. Every staff member has a specific role to play. Each person contributes to the function and integrity of their workplace. Like a cancer or infection, malfunction in any part of the business, down to the level of the individual, can contribute to the demise or extinction of the business.

An extreme example of an organisation brought down by an individual is Barings Bank, which until it closed its doors had been the oldest investment bank in Britain, having operated for over 200 years. The activities of a single employee, a senior derivatives trader named Nick Leeson, led to the bank's collapse in 1995 with a loss of $1.4 billion. Leeson had been seen as the golden child, brilliant at creating money for the bank, which turned a blind eye to his super-speculative and unauthorised dealings.

Building organisational health need not be hard. It requires putting in place the checks and boundaries, ensuring everyone shares the same set of values, beliefs and purpose in support of creating a successful business. It implies having regular organisational health check-ups as a normal part of maintaining good workplace health. It's about nurturing the minds of every individual so they feel valued, respected and motivated, which is what drives engagement.

It also means a change in what a business chooses to invest in when looking to create continuing and successful change for the future.

Investing in mental capital

Traditionally companies have typically invested a great deal in buying the latest technology to stay up to date and competitive. Similarly, it has been expected that the management of staff expertise would include investment in further training and hiring of new staff with particular skills.

This is of course a huge cost to business, but one seen as essential. What has previously been overlooked has been any consideration of how to better manage the staff's existing mental capital. If your company has a number of talented individuals, hired for their particular expertise, who are not working to their capacity, this is a huge waste of human talent and a missed opportunity to accelerate their potential — and therefore the growth of the company.

The view has been that the soft stuff — how people are managed within the workplace — was somehow less relevant or important to the business than the technical knowledge.

This view might have been applicable in the industrial era, but it has no place in the modern workplace.

The human species has been so remarkably successful because of both our ability to adapt to change in our environment and our ability to connect with each other. We are social beings, hardwired to flourish through working and living with others. It is our relationships that matter above everything else — the relationships we have with our family and friends, our acquaintances and work colleagues.

In business, relationships with customers are only one facet of the social web of connection we enjoy. Our future success and happiness as individuals and organisations depends on our ability to form, nurture and maintain our relationships.

The companies that understand the importance of this will be the ones that will grow through the development of a culture that is brain friendly, a culture that values and respects all brains at work.

Today the pace of change and the introduction of new ideas and technology is so fast it can be difficult to find the time to absorb and assimilate what could be most useful to us before the next round of advances and upgrades arrive on our doorstep. Which is why it can sometimes be tempting to keep the door closed, bunker down and hope everyone will leave you alone until you are ready to come up and draw breath.

Choosing to invest in the mental capital and wellbeing of every staff member is the obvious path to responsible organisational health. The Foresight Mental Capital and Wellbeing Project produced by the Government Office for Science in London concludes:

> If we are to prosper and thrive in our changing society and in an increasingly interconnected and competitive world, both our mental and material resources will be

vital. Encouraging and enabling everyone to realise their potential throughout their lives will be crucial for our future prosperity and wellbeing …

An individual's mental capital and mental wellbeing crucially affect their path through life. Moreover, they are vitally important for the healthy functioning of families, communities and society. Together, they fundamentally affect behaviour, social cohesion, social inclusion, and our prosperity.

What is implied is that as individuals we can expect to take greater responsibility for our own health and wellbeing, as well as ensuring that our needs and agendas are being appropriately taken care of in our lives and at work. From an organisation's viewpoint this is about developing greater inclusivity, responsiveness and openness to conversations around performance and development.

So what is *mental capital*?

The Foresight group defines it as the combination of cognitive ability (mental flexibility and efficiency) and emotional intelligence (dealing effectively with stress, resilience and social skills). They define *mental wellbeing* as a dynamic state in which an individual can develop their potential, build strong and positive relationships, and contribute to the community.

Mental capital implies a value base, which ties in nicely with the idea that brains matter and that growing brains to work at their best makes perfect economic sense.

Growing healthy workplaces leads to high performance.

'Organisational health,' writes Patrick Lencioni in his book *The Advantage*, 'will one day surpass all other disciplines in business as the greatest opportunity for improvement and competitive advantage.' He defines organisational health as the integration of management, operations, strategy and culture. Sure, business needs strategy, marketing, finance and technology, but it also needs to deal with those people issues poisoning so many workplaces:

» bullying

» micromanagement

» poor communication or, worse still, lack of communication

» confusion around expectation

» silo mentality

» change resistance

» lack of trust

» lack of relatedness

» lack of collaboration

» lack of innovation

» lack of effective leadership.

I could go on, but I think you get the drift. There is a lot of 'sickness' in many of today's workplaces, which ultimately leads to a loss of integrity and organisational health.

Lencioni is right. Restoring organisational health has to start with going back to the basics of creating a healthy brain capable of consistently thinking well, with less effort, even when under pressure. People today live and work under an incredible amount of pressure. Having to juggle multiple, often complex tasks with the perception of time poverty stresses us out. This in turn can compromise mental performance.

Organisational health is about making sure that:

» you feel you have the capability to do your work and do it well

» you can enjoy what you spend so much of your time doing

» you feel you have enough time and energy at the end of the day to devote to those things that give you pleasure and mean most to you.

Media business commentators such as Alan Kohler in Australia love to discuss the reasons why various businesses are or are not performing well. A commentator will note the links between profit margins, profit forecasts and ASX performance, but until fairly recently there has been little research into which specific elements of human behaviour contribute to high performance.

A study published by the Society for Knowledge Economics in 2011 revealed some fascinating insights into what makes the biggest difference to how well a business performs. Cutting through all the business-speak, Steven Vamos, President of the Society for Knowledge Economics, summarised their findings nicely:

> The study shows that leaders in higher performing organisations prioritise people management as a key priority, involve their people in decision making processes; are more responsive to customer and stakeholder needs; encourage a high degree of responsiveness to change and learning orientation, and enable their staff to fully use their skills and abilities at work.

> High performing organisations are not just much more profitable and productive, they also perform better in many important "intangible attributes", such as encouraging innovation, leadership of their people, and creating a fair workplace environment.

From the survey of 5601 employees from 78 Australian organisations who participated in this study, it was revealed that the highest performing workplaces enjoyed a 12 per cent higher level of productivity, which translated into a profit margin roughly three times higher than found in low-performing workplaces.

The key differences were all derived from human interaction and behaviour.

How we think and how we work as a consequence are hugely influenced by our mood, health and interactions with others.

IT'S TRUE. WE ARE HUMANS WHO THINK AND FEEL. IT'S TIME TO PUT THE HUMANITY BACK INTO HOW WE CHOOSE TO LIVE OUR LIVES AND DO OUR WORK.

The 12 keys to developing a high-performance brain

The currency of the digi-age is our mental capital and well-being. We have lived through a number of different eras: the agricultural age, the industrial age, the technological age — and now we sit squarely in the Age of Appquarius. It's also the age of the brain and thinking, when the human brain will differentiate itself through imagination, innovation and creativity.

Today it's important to ask what changes you wish to see, and how you can achieve them in the context of under-standing that:

» change is hard and the brain resists it

» effective change in a global economy requires all of our social, emotional and cultural intelligences to work collaboratively

» changing how we relate to and communicate with others at an interpersonal level is required to boost collaboration.

This is why organisational health and intelligence must be managed now for organisational survival. Economic conditions are tight, the marketplace is noisy with increasing global competition, and confidence remains low. We can't imagine the speed at which our future brain will operate, or the speed of future change. But the pace of change will continue to challenge us, so we will have to adapt fast, and in the right way to keep up.

What we do know about change is this:

» It's happening all around us. It is normal, expected and often desired.

» It's neverending. Change invariably leads to further change.

» It's tiring. Too often, change strategy takes a lot of effort and distracts from other important work on hand, which can lead to change fatigue.

» It isn't always for the good. Knowing how to differentiate the good from the bad or the ugly is sometimes hard, and it can often not be determined until tested. There will always be an element of risk involved.

» It can be hard work.

However, change is essential as an adaptive process that leads to growth and opportunity. People sometimes talk about change management, but change isn't 'managed' at all. It is chaotic and ever evolving. Instead of managing it we need to *lead* it — and to lead it courageously.

While change has always been with us, its trajectory and pace have reached levels never previously experienced. That's not to say we can't keep up, but we do face a big challenge. Every generation reflects fondly on 'the good old days', when the world was simpler and moved at a slower pace. The reality is that people in the good old days would have felt the pressures of change too.

Just how much the pace of change has accelerated is reflected in the fact that the average person has more information at their fingertips today than the president of the United States had 20 years ago. The Ten Pound Poms took six weeks to reach Australia by boat. Today the flight between London and Perth takes around 19 hours. First-class post was deemed worth the extra cost of getting your letter to its destination a day or so sooner. Today we exchange information and news in a matter of seconds with just a few keystrokes.

That's why going back to the basics of understanding how to create a fit and healthy brain has to be the starting point of any new development. Getting the foundations right first (see figure A) means it's then far easier to evolve towards operational excellence.

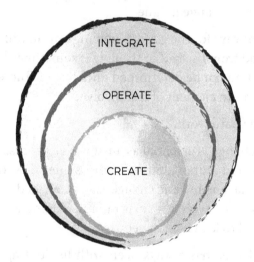

Figure A: the three parts of a high-performance brain

Part I of *Smarter Sharper Thinking* (the first four chapters) is devoted to creating a fitter, healthier brain based on the key lifestyle choices of nutrition, exercise, sleep and flexing our mental muscle.

Part II examines how we can operate at a higher level by addressing how we focus, how we can actively choose our mindset, how to stress 'right' and how to notice more.

In part III we look at how our relationships integrate our understanding of how to be more changeable, innovative, collaborative and effective in leading others and ourselves.

The benefits of creating our own high-performance brain include regaining a sense of control, better managing our time, and gaining a greater sense of achievement and overall happiness. Being simply happy — not deliriously ecstatic, but rather experiencing a quiet contentment connecting us to a deeper sense of purpose and meaning (see figure B) — is no longer such a common experience.

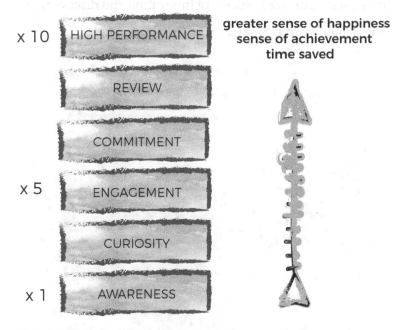

Figure B: getting to a high-performance brain

If you are aware that you are not performing at your best, or you want to increase your brain's ability to engage and innovate, this book is designed to assist you in your strategic thinking. You have been smart enough to come this far, so you are already on the right path to high-performance thinking!

My hope is that this book will open your eyes to the wonder and magic of your own brain (see figure C). While the 12 keys will be explored separately, each adds synergistically to the others. Not every key will be of equal relevance to you. Once you have established the foundations of a brain-healthy lifestyle, I suggest you focus on those elements you believe will most help you to create, operate and enjoy the benefits of a high-performance brain. It is your choice. Yours.

Remember, like any form of evolution, your smarter sharper thinking brain education should never stop. Like the age we live in, it is a constant process of innovation and discovery.

Welcome to your Smarter Sharper Thinking.

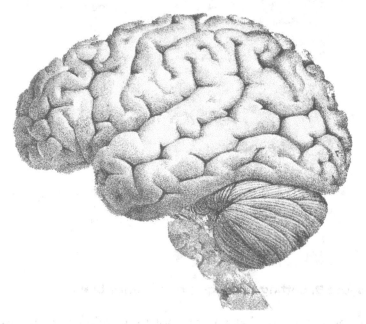

Figure C: the human brain

Part I
Creating a high-performance brain

KEY 1
Nutrition
Refuelling smart

'To eat is a necessity, but to eat intelligently is an art.'
Francois de La Rochefoucauld

Think of your brain as a car and your body as a highway. Would you prefer to be driving a brand new Ferrari, or a rust bucket leaking oil and coughing smoke all over the road?

If your brain was a car, and you knew it needed fuel, what sort of fuel would you choose? Premium high octane, economy or diesel? What sort of car would you drive? Would you look after it, washing, waxing and cleaning it on weekends, or would you be one of those people who smoked on the way to work and left lolly wrappers and food crumbs all over the seats?

Substitute your brain for the car. How well do you fuel your brain? Are you eating clean, or is every night a frenzy of fast food and fizzy drinks? Then there's alcohol ...

Paleo, Pritikin and Pizza Hut aside, we now know from years of nutritional research that our choice of foods can influence:

» our memory

» our general cognitive skills

3

» our mood

» our mental health

» our ability to perform well in the workplace

» even our potential risk of brain disease.

We eat because we are hungry, because we are bored or to be social. We eat for pleasure or because we are miserable. We sometimes even eat because we are forced to (remember those dreaded cold brussels sprouts from childhood?).

What we are often blissfully unaware of however, is the influence that the many different physiological, psychological, social and environmental factors have on determining the how, what and when of our eating. These in turn impact our decision making and, importantly for many of us, our business outcomes.

So how do we keep our brains in optimal physical condition? In the Neuron Grand Prix, what needs to happen to claim podium position?

Brainy facts about nutrition and work

» Our brain is an energy hog that consumes 20 per cent of all the energy we put into our body. Providing sufficient energy through an array of proteins, fats and carbohydrates is essential for good cognitive performance and health.

» We can go without food for a while, but water is essential to healthy thinking. Even 1 per cent dehydration is associated with fuzzy thinking, so keep up your fluid intake with six to eight glasses of water every day.

> » Caffeine keeps us awake and alert. Some studies have shown it also helps the formation of long-term memory following study.
>
> » There is no single best diet or food. Following a brain-healthy eating pattern incorporates certain aspects of the Mediterranean diet and sticking to 'real food'. It's about including a wide variety of fresh, unprocessed foods, vegetables and fruits, lean protein (including three portions of oily fish each week), seeds, nuts and whole grains.
>
> » Our food choices determine our mood and contribute to our mental wellbeing and focus. Avoiding processed foods full of fat and sugar is the best way to maintain healthy cognition.

You're such a fathead

The human brain is around 60 per cent fat, so the next time you call someone a fathead, they are well within their rights to say, 'Same to you'. Consuming the right fats to sustain our brain's function and maintain our neural architecture is absolutely critical to functional integrity and brain performance.

The brain can produce its own cholesterol, but we rely entirely on our dietary intake of essential fatty acids (omega-3) to create neurotransmitters and keep neuronal membranes flexible for optimal brain function.

Low levels of omega-3 may cause your brain to age faster. Studies by ZS Tan and others using MRI scans and memory tests showed that those in the lowest 25th percentile for omega-3 consumption had smaller brain volumes and scored lower on memory, abstract thinking and problem solving.

An imbalance or overconsumption of bad fats changes the brain and contributes to poorer brain performance. Research has linked trans fats, as found in margarines, fast foods, baked snacks, biscuits, pies and frozen pizza, to poorer memory in young and middle-aged men. As Beatrice Golumb expresses it, 'Trans fats increase the shelf life of foods and reduce the shelf life of people'. For those in the earlier part of their career, where performance matters, paying attention to food choices can make a difference.

Dr Golumb's study found the following:

» Men under the age of 45 who ate more trans fats performed worse on word memory tests, even after taking into account variables of age, education, ethnicity and depression.

» Each additional gram of trans fat consumed was associated with an estimated 0.76 fewer words correctly recalled.

» Those eating the highest amount of trans fats overall showed a 10 per cent reduction in words remembered compared with those adults who ate the least trans fats.

Gut instinct

Everyone knows the saying 'trust your gut'. But is this actually good advice, not just in relation to our business instincts, but when it comes to what we like to eat?

Our food choices have been shown to affect how we feel. If we are unhappy at work, we sometimes seek consolation through eating — and what we choose to eat then is often not good food. We go for 'comfort foods', high in trans fats and refined sugar, which provide an instant high, followed by a big crash and burn, leading to a further drop in mood and energy.

Food choice matters because it determines mood and performance. One Spanish study of more than 12000 subjects (average age 37 years), followed over a six-year period, revealed that those consuming a diet highest in trans fats had a risk of depression that was 48 per cent higher than those who consumed the least trans fats. Yes, not everyone in Mediterranean countries necessarily follows a healthy Mediterranean diet!

Medically, this finding is explained by the fact that trans fats stimulate a higher level of inflammation in the body, increasing the risk of fatty plaques being laid down and interference with the brain's neurotransmitters concerned with regulating mood.

Conversely, enjoying a diet higher in omega-3s, the fatty acids essential for good brain health and function as found in oily fish, has been shown to be associated with a lower risk of depression and cognitive decline.

So *should* we trust our gut when deciding what we feel like putting in our stomachs?

The answer is, not necessarily!

We have what is called a gut microbiome, a diverse bacterial population that lives in our gut. These bacteria can direct our brain's food choices to suit their survival needs, although we can counterbalance this through healthy food choices to change the gut microflora so as to stay healthier both physically and mentally.

FAT IS NOT ALWAYS UGLY

Not all fats are bad fats. Cholesterol, which has typically been portrayed as the Dr Evil of the fat world, is essential to the brain for synaptogenesis (the formation of new synapses) and hence critical for brain plasticity, learning and memory. Saturated fats, as found in meat, dairy, nuts and olive oil, benefit brain function when consumed in moderation.

Our brain has a very special relationship with cholesterol. The brain synthesises its own, retaining it and effectively shielding it from the rest of the body behind the blood–brain barrier. Twenty-five per cent of the body's total cholesterol is found in the brain, mostly as myelin, the fatty coating around nerve cells that speeds up the transmission of electrical impulses.

Cholesterol is needed also for the formation of dopaminergic neurons, involved in our brain's reward response system and motivation. Feeling good and being mentally rewarded for our efforts are critical for maintaining engagement and performance.

MINDING YOUR MIND INCLUDES MINDING YOUR WEIGHT

Obesity shrinks the brain. It reduces brain volume. It is also a risk factor for cognitive decline. With 30 per cent of the world's population either overweight or obese, there are now more than 2.1 billion people at risk of cognitive decline through this factor alone.

Having a smaller brain volume affects brain function (see figure 1.1):

» in the hippocampus, the area of the brain associated with learning and memory

» in the frontal lobes, the area associated with higher-level thinking, including paying attention, planning and organising

» in the anterior cingulate gyrus, the area associated with decision making, empathy and emotion

» in the thalamus, the area associated with coordinating other areas of brain function.

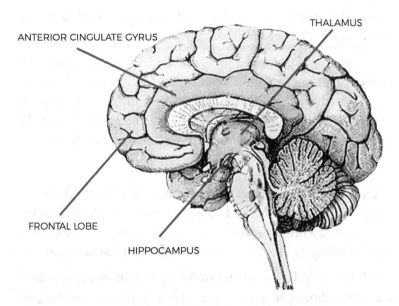

THALAMUS

ANTERIOR CINGULATE GYRUS

FRONTAL LOBE

HIPPOCAMPUS

Figure 1.1: parts of the brain affected by obesity

Obesity affects our cognition because greater effort is required to complete complex decision-making tasks. Encouraging all staff to watch their weight not only helps them to stay fitter and healthier; it is a way to maintain their cognition.

Food and focus

We reach our cognitive peak for motor performance around the lofty age of 24. But before you slump into a deep depression about being 'over the hill', although your speed of processing may have slowed down, your increasing ability to use your experience and growing wisdom enables your brain to take a few mental shortcuts.

It's a bit like discovering the disguised cut-throughs that enable you to escape the Ikea store more quickly without having to follow the illuminated arrows for the 30 kilometres required to reach the checkout, when all you wanted was to buy a nice new office lamp.

A study in 2014 by Thompson and others analysed the influence of age on performance in 3035 players (aged 16 to 44) of the video game *StarCraft II* and found that while cognitive motor decline starts early, it is compensated for by the continuing adaptability of our massively plastic brain.

Hurrah!

One of the things we want to be able to do at work is focus on what matters, so we stay on task and get our work done. In some instances, the modern workplace seems to conspire against us by presenting us with ever-increasing levels of distraction.

We can help boost our focus by paying attention to which foods we choose to eat. It really is as simple as focusing on eating 'real food'. The following foods have been shown in nutritional studies to assist in boosting focus, and this list is by no means exhaustive. Just think of fresh, minimally processed foods and you will be on the right track, but consider especially:

» leafy greens — kale, spinach, Chinese broccoli, chard and other dark leafy greens

» whole grains — oats, couscous, brown rice, rye, barley and (for those who can tolerate gluten) wheat

» coffee — two or three cups of coffee each day to keep us awake, alert and primed to pay attention

» berries — especially the deeply pigmented blue and red fruits, such as blueberries, cherries, plums, strawberries and raspberries

» cold-water, oily carnivorous fish — wild salmon, herring, mackerel, pilchards, sardines and anchovies

» nuts and seeds — walnuts, almonds, flaxseed, sunflower seeds

» dark chocolate — minimum 70 per cent cocoa solids, preferably the best you can find, because here it's quality, not quantity, that matters

» eggs — choline boosts focus and helps to reduce cortisol, one of our stress hormones.

PRIMING THE PUMP

As mentioned, the brain consumes 20 per cent of the energy we use each day, despite comprising only 2 per cent of our body mass. Like a credit card with a high interest rate, it's for the best if we keep it in the black. People who skip breakfast have greater activity in the pleasure-seeking part of the brain and are more easily seduced by pictures of high-calorie food. Skipping breakfast means you are more susceptible to that advert for Subway or McDonald's you pass on your way to work.

When we skip meals, our neurons, which rely on glucose as their primary energy source, have to break down stores from elsewhere. That's why it's better to have a handy supply of snacks such as fruit, a handful of nuts or some crackers to get you through a busy thinking time so you can maintain your cognitive stamina and focus.

Paradoxically, intermittent fasting has a positive impact on our biochemical balance, improving insulin sensitivity and lowering peripheral cholesterol. Skipping an occasional meal is not a problem and can help with weight loss or maintenance.

Overall, providing our brain with a steady supply of oxygen and appropriate nutrients is the best way to keep it fuelled up for best performance.

If you've been wondering whether hunger and fatigue really make that much difference to outcomes, the answer is yes they do. If you've got to focus over a long period of time, taking regular brain breaks and having a meal or a snack replenishes your ability to keep making decisions.

Avoiding decision fatigue matters. Think about those times at work when running out of mental juice could potentially alter your decision making and outcomes. That's why important decisions should not be made late in the day.

STOCKING UP ON WILLPOWER

Every time we make a decision, big or small, we exert willpower — and our daily stock of willpower is not infinite. With around 30 000 decisions to be made every day, it's easy to see how our cognitive energy can be depleted over the course of the day. Self-control principally involves the prefrontal cortex and is hugely energy demanding. Avoiding confused thinking in the workplace resulting from low glucose levels is essential from a health and safety perspective.

The ramifications of poor decisions may impact more than just the hungry person involved. It could spell the loss of a job, a client or even a business.

We can recover willpower and cognitive stamina through the simple act of eating something to restore the glucose supply our neurons need to start firing again. A study by Roy Baumeister and John Tierney showed how drinking one glass of sweet lemonade can produce the desired effect. (Artificially sweetened lemonade doesn't produce the same improvement.) But sugary drinks are not the answer in the 'real world'. Animal studies have shown that adolescents who drink sugar-sweetened drinks daily show increased inflammation of the hippocampus, the area of the brain associated with learning and memory, leading to an impaired ability to learn and remember.

The Western diet is often high in added sugar. Worldwide consumption has tripled over the past 50 years. This is associated with the rapid escalation in the global incidence of obesity and type 2 diabetes, both risk factors for cognitive decline and dementia. Animal studies have shown that having too high blood glucose levels affects insulin receptors in the brain, leading to a dulling of spatial learning and memory. Choosing to consume fewer foods that are high in sugar and to increase fibre and protein intake along with omega-3 supplements appears to partially negate this effect.

We obtain the glucose we need from the carbohydrates found in fruits and vegetables, so eating a small banana instead of a sugary snack will do the trick, as will snacking on blueberries, shown in studies to boost memory and concentration for up to five hours.

Creating a workplace culture that discourages (rather than bans) soft drinks and sugary snacks, leading by example, is one way to assist all brains at work to stay healthy and function better.

The java jive

The world's most widely consumed psychostimulant is caffeine. We drink it in our coffee, tea and energy drinks. We eat it as chocolate. We love our caffeine because it gives us a buzz, it keeps us alert and we enjoy the taste.

When first established in the 17th century, European coffee houses became meeting places and powerhouses of intellectual discussion. Perhaps we cannot make the same claim of our cafés and coffee outlets today, yet many business meetings revolve around meeting up for a coffee.

WE USE COFFEE TO KEEP US ALERT, BUT DOES IT ACTUALLY IMPROVE PERFORMANCE?

The short answer is no, it makes no difference overall, *except* when it comes to learning and forming long-term memory. A study published in *Nature Neuroscience* in 2014 showed that timing is everything here. Drinking a coffee (or tea) *after* learning something enhances memory consolidation. So treating yourself to your daily java after the lecture or training course is finished is the way to go!

Just remember, too high a dose of caffeine will start to disrupt working memory performance through the overstimulation effect. Caffeine increases the rate of neuronal firing, which would seem beneficial but quickly leads to cognitive exhaustion and the feeling we need another cup.

The recommended maximum intake of caffeine is 400 mg a day, or about three cups of coffee. There is a wide spectrum of individual sensitivity, however, and too much caffeine can make you feel jittery or lead to heart palpitations.

There have been a number of deaths reported from overconsumption of caffeine, usually in the form of 'energy' drinks. These innocuous-tasting drinks can contain very high levels of caffeine, which, when consumed in large amounts over a short period of time, can lead in susceptible individuals to unstable heart rhythms and tachycardia (rapid heartbeat). According to the University of New South Wales (cited by ABC Health and Wellbeing), per-drink caffeine levels are as a rule of thumb (depending on the length of time of brew and the type of tea or coffee beans):

» one cup of barista-style coffee contains 40 to 90 mg caffeine

» one cup of instant coffee contains 60 to 100 mg

» one cup of black, green or white tea contains 30 to 100 mg

Among the energy drinks:

» Red Bull contains 80 mg per 250 mL

» Mother contains 160 mg per 500 mL can.

You might think, well, Mother has no more caffeine per millilitre than Red Bull. The issue is that once the can is open, of course you are more likely to drink all of it!

It doesn't take much to reach that recommended daily limit of 400 mg. But by staying close to an average of two to three cups of coffee a day, you won't be putting yourself at any particular risk of harm to your health.

OTHER BRAINY BENEFITS OF COFFEE DRINKING INCLUDE A LOWER RISK OF DEMENTIA AND, ACCORDING TO THE NURSES' HEALTH STUDY OF OVER 50 000 WOMEN, A LOWER RISK OF DEPRESSION.

Our daily desk

Carl Honoré believes eating well is a lost art. 'Food is often little more than fuel to pour down the hatch while doing other stuff — surfing the Web, driving, walking along the street. Dining "al desko" is now the norm in many workplaces. All of this speed takes a toll. Obesity, eating disorders and poor nutrition are rife.'

It may not be appropriate for workplaces to regulate what their staff eat, but promoting a work culture that endorses healthy nutrition makes sense, especially as we spend two-thirds of our lives there. Leading by example means that everyone from the CEO down stops for lunch and takes appropriate refuelling breaks mid morning and afternoon, and that healthy food choices are made readily accessible.

The Association of UK Dieticians has put in place 'Nutrition in the Workplace', a service providing nutrition workshops such as 'Good mood food' and 'How to sustain yourself through a busy working day'. In addition they provide one-on-one nutrition clinic days.

Nutrition Australia runs a similar workplace health and wellbeing program, providing information and education to companies in the form of nutrition seminars; cooking demonstrations; lunch 'n' learns; menu, catering and vending machine assessments; one-on-one consults; and customised programs.

THE QUESTION IS, WITH GROWING KNOWLEDGE OF HOW IMPORTANT NUTRITION IS TO OUR MOOD, WELLBEING AND PERFORMANCE, CAN WE AFFORD THE CONSEQUENCES OF POOR NUTRITIONAL CHOICES?

TIME IS MONEY

When feeling time poor and under the pump or chasing deadlines, we are not focused on making the best food choices. We make do by eating on the run, grabbing whatever food is available, which is typically fast foods laden with fat, salt and sugar. Indulging in poor nutritional choices at the very time when you require your best thinking skills leads to poorer performance and poorer decisions.

The outcome? A downturn for our bottom line.

There are many reasons why it makes good business sense to promote healthy workplace nutrition:

» It boosts overall health and vitality.

» It boosts productivity and performance.

» It reduces absenteeism and sick leave rates associated with chronic health problems.

» It reduces the costs associated with:

  » higher levels of sick pay

  » disability associated with chronic health conditions

  » early retirement.

A healthy workforce is a healthy business.

We need good food:

» for stamina — to provide us with the fuel we need to get us through our long working day

» for focus — to help us pay attention to what matters, learn and remember

» for a positive mood — to raise confidence and competence, and foster a balanced approach to our tasks

» for better cognition — for problem solving, decision making, innovation and insight.

FEED YOUR BRAIN

It's all about the right fuel for the right vehicle.

A multitude of eating plans and diets are promoted, each of whose authors tout their particular program as inherently superior to all others. Some have a scientific basis; others are more faddish. Extreme examples will not only give your brain a big fat headache but can be dangerous to your general health.

But is there one superior brainy diet? In 2014 Katz and Meller compared the medical evidence for and against all the current mainstream diets, to see if one really did have the edge over another. What they discovered was that the solution to great health comes from what they term 'real food'.

While many eating plans have merits, whether you choose to follow a vegetarian, vegan macrobiotic, raw, gluten-free or just plain fussy diet doesn't matter, so long as your chosen way of eating provides your brain and body with all the essential nutrients it needs to stay healthy.

Rather than following the latest fashion trend of over-proscriptive, regimented eating plans, healthy eating starts by including healthier alternatives. If it's fresh, locally sourced and unprocessed, chances are it will be a healthy food. And making a series of small changes is easier to adapt to for the longer term.

If in doubt, remember that 'diet' is simply an acronym for 'Do I eat this?'

The eating plan that has consistently been shown by multiple studies to be good for the brain (and is of course taken for granted by the people of the region!) is that followed by the communities that have lived around the Mediterranean for centuries. This diet comprises green leafy vegetables, lean protein (especially cold-water, oily, carnivorous fish), seeds and nuts, whole grains, deeply pigmented fruits, olive oil and red wine (in moderate amounts).

Studies by Georgios Tsivgoulis and others have reported those without diabetes who followed the Mediterranean diet more closely had a 19 per cent lower risk of developing memory and thinking difficulties compared with those following a more typical Western diet that is considerably higher in trans fats, saturated fats and sugar.

Excluding certain food types — going 'low-carb' or 'sugar-free', for example — isn't the way to a balanced diet. Neither will swallowing a bucketload of vitamins and minerals provide you with the cognitive edge you may be looking for. Even the so-called brain 'super foods' are insufficient on their own. While adding in some extra turmeric, cacao and fish oil may be useful, they don't provide a lot of benefit in isolation.

In a nutshell, synthetic vitamins and supplements by themselves can never deliver the same benefits to be found in the unique synergy of elements that real food provides.

That's not to say having snack foods or fast food occasionally is going to be detrimental — as long as these foods are an occasional treat rather than staples.

THE QUICKEST WAY TO COMPLETELY STUFF UP OUR BRAINS IS TO STUFF OUR BODIES WITH FAST FOOD.

The excuses we make to ourselves for not choosing healthy foods are the obstacles we put in our own path. What we're really saying is, 'I don't want to invest the time in changing how I do things'.

Tips for building brain nutrition at work

For the individual

I'm just too busy to stop and eat.

Taking the time to pause and replenish your brain's fuel stores will increase efficiency and help you get your work done better and faster.

I don't have time to stand in line and wait to buy lunch.

Pre-ordering can save time, or bring lunch with you to work. Preparing a nutritious salad, wrap or roll need only take a couple of minutes in the morning.

The cafeteria only serves hot chips and deep-fried food.

As above, but maybe it's time to have a chat with management about introducing some healthy food alternatives at work.

When I'm really stressed and under the pump, I tend to gravitate to fast food and carbs.

Being aware of how we respond to stress allows us to be prepared with some healthy snacks such as a banana or a small packet of nuts, which makes it easier to forgo the donut or pizza alternative.

If we're all working late and someone orders in takeaway, I don't like to be difficult.

What we do occasionally isn't the problem. So unless working late is the rule and this is an office ritual, sometimes it's better to go with the flow and choose healthier options at other times.

For the organisation

Leadership starts by example:

» If the CEO and senior execs are seen to take appropriate meal breaks and make healthy food choices, it demonstrates an appreciation of the importance of maintaining health and vitality.

» Provide fresh water that is readily accessible to all staff, to keep brains hydrated and working well.

» Vending machines that provide healthy snacks and drinks are great for busy people and will be appreciated.

» Keep fresh fruit (instead of cookies) on view in a bowl or in the fridge in an office kitchen.

» Provide safe food storage for those bringing food into the workplace.

» Accommodate those with special dietary needs. As with many restaurants and cafés, including vegetarian, gluten-free and lactose-free options, for example, means everyone is included in a brain-friendly nutrition environment.

» An in-house cafeteria is the ideal place to provide wholesome meals at a reasonable cost, creating a social hub where people can enjoy their meal break while catching up with colleagues.

» Educational sessions led by accredited nutritionists can provide nutritional advice and practical ideas in lunch'n'learns.

» Information brochures outlining healthy food options and nutrition policies in the workplace can reinforce the message that healthy eating is encouraged.

» Discourage 'al desko' eating by making it a policy that meal breaks be taken away from the desk. Encouraging all staff to take regular meal and brain breaks rather than 'working through' promotes a healthy working brain culture and higher performance.

» When catering for in-house meetings and conference sessions, use providers that offer a variety of healthy options, including platters of fresh fruit, salads and vegetables.

KEY 2
Exercise
You've got to move it, move it

In the first key, we compared your brain to a car. Now if you have any fondness for F1, you will be aware that there aren't many overweight drivers squeezing themselves into the cockpit of a McLaren or Ferrari to roar around a Grand Prix circuit. If they were carrying much excess flesh, first, they wouldn't fit, but second, the stress on their bodies would compromise their ability to make high-performance decisions in a split second. Lewis Hamilton gained the nickname of 'Chubby' when he was not doing so well in the rankings. Coincidence?

There's one thing that *every* future brain needs. The research shows it to make by far the biggest impact on our cognition, mental flexibility, memory, mood and wellbeing. It's so powerful, nothing comes close to offering the benefits it provides.

It's the one thing pharmaceutical companies would love to get their hands on and patent, because they would become instant squillionaires. They can't, though, because it can never be produced as a potion or a pill. You can't rub it on or take it as a supplement. But it does need to be taken daily.

What is it?

You've probably guessed. It's called *exercise*.

Yes, good old-fashioned exercise, the physical sort, has been shown to help optimise how well your brain works for you by strengthening existing neural networks, promoting neuroplasticity (the production of new synaptic connections) and neurogenesis (the production of new neurons).

Brainy facts about working out and the workplace

» Exercise enhances blood flow to the brain, leading to reduced brain shrinkage and increased neurogenesis and plasticity, so your work performance stays top notch.

» It provides improved cognition, learning and memory.

» It improves mood and self-esteem, reduces stress, and reduces the risk of anxiety and depression.

» It improves heart and circulatory health associated with a lower risk of heart attack, high blood pressure or stroke.

» There is a decreased risk of cognitive impairment and lower risk of cognitive decline and neurodegenerative disease.

Business on the move

Exercise brings benefits to businesses, large and small, that are immeasurable in terms of employee wellbeing — and highly measurable in terms of the bottom line. Brains that work out work better and last longer. We feel more energised, competent and confident. Exercise helps us to manage our heavy workloads, think faster on our feet and enjoy greater mental agility.

In its 2013–14 Staying@Work Survey Report, Towers Watson identified stress (78 per cent), lack of physical exercise (73 per cent) and obesity (75 per cent) as the top health issues listed by employers. Increasing physical activity at work naturally helps to resolve the other two issues.

Business wellness programs offer far more than just improved health and wellbeing. The cognitive edge gained through exercise and increased wellness is rewarded by higher staff retention, lower rates of absenteeism and presenteeism, greater productivity, higher morale and greater loyalty to the organisation.

Far from being a 'nice to have' value-add, investment in employee wellbeing is now recognised by brain-savvy businesses as making good business sense on many levels:

» A study by Katherine Baikler and others revealed in the US every dollar invested in health and wellbeing has an ROI of $5.82 in reduced absenteeism costs.

» According to a study by Dishman and others, workplace health programs have been shown to reduce sick leave by 30 per cent, increase productivity by 52 per cent and reduce workers compensation and disability costs by 32 per cent.

» Exercise lifts levels of engagement, focus and application to the work performed — and lifts the bottom line.

» The company gets a public image boost, being seen as caring for the health and wellbeing of its staff, which increases its attraction as a place to work.

Despite the image of the bronzed and sports-loving Aussie, even though we're so often portrayed as fit and buff lifesavers, Ironmen, footy players and cricketers, the reality is the vast majority of the population prefers to sit and watch rather than participate in sport.

But it's not just an Australian problem. While 70 per cent of Australians are not physically active enough to maintain good health, 80 per cent of American adults don't get the recommended amount of exercise each week.

Self-reported statistics in the UK found 67 per cent of men and 55 per cent of women claimed that they fulfilled the recommendations for aerobic activity, but it seems, as is often the case, what they believed they were doing didn't come close to matching the reality. Objective measures of these fitness levels found 70 per cent of men and 80 per cent of women fell below their age-appropriate activity level.

The size of the problem reflects not only how inactive we have become, but the lost potential and profit that a healthy, active workforce can offer.

THE FACT IS WE THINK BETTER AFTER WE EXERCISE.

Functional MRI (fMRI) studies by Sandra Chapman and others have shown how exercise leads to increased blood flow to two key areas in the brain, the anterior cingulate and the hippocampus (see figure 2.1).

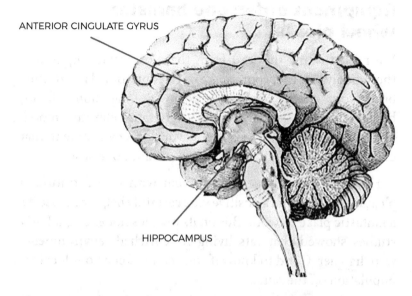

ANTERIOR CINGULATE GYRUS

HIPPOCAMPUS

Figure 2.1: exercise increases cerebral blood flow

The anterior cingulate has three main functions: first, it's an error detector that helps us spot when something is different about our environment; second, it's involved in how we prepare and anticipate task performance; and third, it is involved in the regulation of our emotions. The hippocampus, meanwhile, relates to spatial learning and memory.

An increase in blood flow indicates increased cerebral metabolism and neuronal activity, with extra oxygen and nutrients being delivered to the brain. This is what leads to better performance. From an evolutionary point of view, keeping your wits about you while running from a predator, for example, may help you escape harm.

Equipment order: one hamster wheel please

We need to take the lead from the kids screaming around the schoolyard. Incorporating exercise into our daily routine boosts our energy levels, sharpens thinking, hones focus, boosts memory, enhances creativity and elevates mood. The challenge lies in creating a working environment that encourages us to be active so we can produce our best.

Having a great office environment with nice furniture, a pleasant outlook and a positive vibe certainly helps, because it's a fantastic place to work. But on its own it's not enough. Early studies showed that rats living in 'enriched' environments were happier. Good to know if you want to keep your local rat population off the sauce.

But happiness apart, it was essential to find out exactly which aspect of an enriched environment made the rats want to stay away from the local bar. Justin Rhodes and his colleagues at the Beckman Institute for Advanced Science and Technology and the University of Illinois decided to find the answer. It turned out not to be about the toys, bells and whistles the rats had to play with.

It was having access to a running wheel.

Installing a running wheel in the office may not be a practical option. It's really about what to invest the workplace budget in that will make the biggest difference to boosting performance. If the choice is between new office furniture and putting in an office gym, I think you know the answer.

Besides increasing blood flow, exercise boosts the release of neurotransmitters in the brain, and this is where the real magic lies. Exercise leads to an increase in the amount of BDNF (brain-derived neurotrophic factor, for short) the brain secretes. John Ratey calls BDNF 'Miracle-Gro' for brains because this is what boosts neuronal health, strengthens synaptic connections and stimulates neurogenesis — the production of new neurons and their incorporation into our existing neural architecture.

In other words, exercise helps us to grow and strengthen our brain, allowing us to learn, remember and recall information better. And to maintain the healthy thinking, innovation and creativity we need to keep moving.

IS THERE AN OPTIMAL TIME TO EXERCISE?

Yes and no. In an ideal world, exercising every morning for 20 to 30 minutes is perfect. That's because exercise is brilliant at increasing blood flow (hence sending extra oxygen and nutrients to specific brain areas) and swooshing extra BDNF around your brain, but the mental results come later.

Exercise is the primer that enables your brain to work at its best (see figure 2.2).

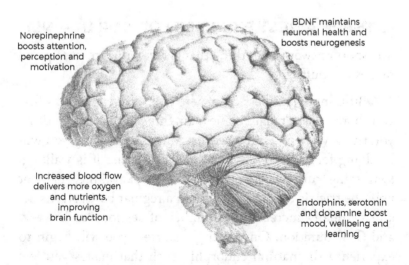

Figure 2.2: exercise primes performance

However, if early-morning exercise doesn't suit your lifestyle, exercising at other times is fine as well. At lunchtime why not book a gym session, go for a jog, walk around the park or maybe practise some yoga. This works especially well if you've got a hard afternoon coming up with back-to-back meetings, a brainstorming session (more on brainstorming later) or a big project to finish that requires ongoing stamina and focus.

Last but not least, exercising after work is a great way to relax and unwind after a long day. It gives your brain breathing space to consolidate thoughts and perhaps come up with new ideas. It also gives you time to transition your focus from work to home.

The only caveat here is don't exercise too close to bedtime (within two or three hours), as it can interfere with the brain's ability to quieten down in preparation for sleep.

The best time for exercise is the time you have available. And let's face it (pardon the pun), if we have time for Facebook, we have time for exercise.

IS THERE A BEST EXERCISE FOR OUR BRAINS?

The short answer is: anything that gets your heart rate up and makes you puff a bit.

A 30-minute-plus session of aerobic exercise is ideal. What you choose doesn't matter. The main thing is to pick something you think you will enjoy, because this is something you will be doing for the rest of your life! So whether it is walking, swimming, running, cycling, table tennis, kayaking, rugby or golf, the trick is to schedule it in on a regular basis, start slow and gradually increase the number of sessions each week, and their duration. Once you get started, you will begin to experience the natural endorphin rush that makes you feel good and motivates you to want to do it again.

Interval training has become all the rage, with many exercise physiologists telling us you can get all the benefits of a longer session in a short, high-intensity burst. That is certainly true for cardiovascular and general fitness, and the latest research supports the idea that this is also true for the brain. For time-poor business owners, workers and executives this is great news.

The current exercise recommendation

- » 150 minutes of aerobic activity each week
- » or five 30-minute sessions
- » or three lots of 10-minute sessions for five days
- » for high-intensity interval training, 75 minutes a week is fine.

Adding in a couple of stretching and strength sessions each week has also been shown to be useful in boosting good cognitive health and function.

THE SOLUTION FOR EXERCISE PHOBIA

If the thought of donning lycra and going to the gym or being asked by a friend to join them for a jog brings you out in a cold sweat, it's okay. The solution is simply to *move more*.

Unless you are a complete couch potato, spending all your days and nights in a reclining or horizontal position, there will be opportunities for you to become more physically active. (Note how much less threatening 'moving more' sounds than the prospect of all that hard, sweaty, uncomfortable exercise.)

MOVING MORE AND EXERCISING MAKES US HAPPY, AND WHEN WE ARE HAPPY WE ARE MORE CONFIDENT OF OUR ABILITIES, MORE ENGAGED WITH WHAT WE ARE DOING, AND MORE OPEN TO ALTERNATIVES AND INNOVATIVE THINKING.

While moving more is a great start, there is no escaping that exercise is the crucial path to staying healthy, both physically and mentally. Ideally, aim for 20 to 30 minutes of moderately intense exercise every day, and two to three sessions of weights or stretching per week. Even just 12 minutes of aerobic activity will boost memory and cognition. So don't just sit there, move!

If you need a little encouragement to keep on keeping on with your exercise program, then plug in some upbeat music you enjoy. There's a very good reason why gyms play music: it stimulates you to persevere a little longer with your session. On a treadmill, your speed will pick up, your endurance will increase and your stride will start to match the beat of the music you're listening to.

Charles Emery, a psychologist at Ohio State University, investigated the difference listening to music during exercise had on mental performance. In a group undergoing rehabilitation following myocardial infarction, he found that those who exercised while listening to music (he chose Vivaldi's *Four Seasons*) performed twice as well in verbal fluency as those who exercised without music. If Vivaldi isn't your thing, choose something that is.

We can walk, run, swim or cycle our way to better brain health and function, and if music helps us get there, so much the better.

The perils of too much sitting

'Above all, do not lose your desire to walk. Every day I walk myself into a state of wellbeing and walk away from every illness.'
Soren Kierkegaard

So when it comes to creating a fitter, healthier future brain, nothing beats exercise. Except, sadly, all that benefit can be lost through the one activity we humans have unfortunately become far too familiar with: sitting.

Sitting disease is a recognised phenomenon that is integral to our modern lifestyle and way of working. It is linked to poor health (increased risk of certain cancers, including bowel cancer; cardiovascular disease; varicose veins; poor posture; neck, back and hip pain; obesity; poorer thinking; and cognitive decline) and a shortened lifespan.

But sitting disease isn't new. The perils of sitting too long for our occupational health was recognised by an Italian physician, Bernardino Ramazzini, in his published work 'Diseases of workers' back in 1713:

> Those who sit at their work and are therefore called "chair workers," such as cobblers and tailors, become bent and hump-backed and hold their heads down like people looking for something on the ground. These workers ... suffer from general ill health and an excessive accumulation of unwholesome humors caused by their sedentary life.

Ramazzini noted how runners (messengers) avoided many of these health problems and was an early advocate of sedentary workers taking an exercise break. Clearly the message has taken a little while to filter through.

You're probably thinking there are far greater threats to your health than sitting for too long. We know, for example,

33

that smoking is also bad for your health, and indeed it is no longer permitted in Australian workplaces. But according to Mayo Clinic cardiologist Martha Grogan, sitting most of the day gives you about the same risk of heart attack as smoking.

For many, sitting is the new smoking.

A study by the American Cancer Society found if you are sitting for more than six hours every day, your chance of dying from *any* cause over the next 15 years is 40 per cent higher than for someone who sits for less, *even if you exercise*. That's right, sitting too long shortens your life by two to three years and is really bad for your brain.

The problem we have today is the far greater proportion of workers who sit for prolonged periods of time for their work.

Have you ever totted up how much time you spend sitting each day? Be honest. Is it four, six, eight hours — or more? It's possible that you may be spending 13 hours sitting each day, far longer than you spend asleep in your bed!

How can this be? For many of us, we start our day by getting up and then sitting down for breakfast (okay, I know some of you do this differently, standing or running out the door, coffee in hand), and then we sit in the car, the bus or the train on our way to work.

Once at work many of us sit at a desk in front of a computer screen all day long, maybe getting up briefly to take lunch (which we sit and eat) then back to our desk to work hard until it's time to go home again. Travelling home we sit in the car, the bus or the train again. We sit to eat our evening meal, and we may then sit while relaxing in front of the TV or doing some work on the computer before bed. It's easy to see how much of our time is consumed by sitting.

According to a study from Vanderbilt University, the average American is sedentary for 7.7 hours each day. The reality is that for many of us this is a gross underestimate. Statistics from the Mayo Clinic indicate that:

» 50 to 70 per cent of people spend more than six hours each day sitting

» 20 to 35 per cent of people spend at least four hours every day sitting watching TV.

STAND UP FOR YOUR BRAIN!

When we sit for long periods (more than three hours at a time), our inactivity leads to reduced blood flow to the brain, and hence less oxygenation and nutrient supply. James A. Levine says that every two hours spent sitting significantly reduces blood flow and sugar levels. This leads to reduced brain activity, particularly in the energy-hungry prefrontal cortex (PFC).

The PFC is the executive suite we use for all that heavy-duty thinking, planning, organising and decision making. With reduced blood flow, we run out of mental juice and feel mentally tired more quickly. Continuing to press on at this stage further compounds the problem. We would be far better off to stop and take a brain break by getting up to stretch and move for 10 to 15 minutes.

Worse still, all that sitting means the exercise we put all that time and effort into may as well not have happened. That's right, prolonged sitting negates *all* the benefits we derive from exercise. Genevieve Healy, who has done a lot of work in this area, reports that 'we have become so sedentary that 30 minutes at the gym may not counteract the detrimental effects of 8, 9, 10 hours of sitting'.

The solution? We *have* to move more.

JOIN THE MOVEMENT

Note that I'm talking about movement here, *not* exercise. Some companies and businesses have become aware of the problem posed by sitting disease and introduced measures such as standing desks, which have become popular recently. Standing by itself helps to increase metabolic activity and is preferable to sitting. But many people dislike standing for too long, or get backache, or find it hard to work while standing. A better solution may be having a desk that allows you to alternate your posture — sitting for some of the time, standing for the rest.

Going beyond the standing desk, there are treadputers: treadmills with an attached workstation and computer. Here, you can set your preferred speed and basically walk while doing your work. I can see how this would be okay for some office work but not for others. Drawing, for example, would be a serious challenge! I can also see how the office jokester would relish being able to 'adjust' a colleague's treadputer speed. Or is that just my suspicious mind at work?

Gretchen Reynolds, in her book *The First Twenty Minutes*, suggests, 'The first twenty minutes of moving around, if someone has been really sedentary, provide most of the health benefits'. Rather than feeling guilty next time you don't get to the gym (again) and your trainers have expired from lack of use, get up and have a stretch, go for a five-minute walk and commit to developing the habit of doing things that involve moving more every day. From there it becomes easier first to start building this into longer sessions and then to 'up' the physical component by walking more briskly. Start small and then look for new opportunities to move more, especially at the beginning of your day.

Moving includes walking. The ideal distance to preserve brain function is to walk around 15 kilometres each week. Walkers grow bigger brains and preserve memory better.

Nilofer Merchant, a walking meeting advocate who holds around four walking meetings every week, finds they allow her to:

» avoid the guilt around allocating other time to exercise instead of being at work or with family.

» listen more effectively because her attention is better focused on the person she is walking with.

» be less distracted by technology such as her mobile phone.

Moving towards a positive thinking space

The statistics around the incidence of mental illness, anxiety and depression in the workplace are, in a word, depressing.

One in five Australian adults is at risk of experiencing an episode of mental illness in any given 12 months. That's 20 per cent of the population.

DEPRESSION AND ANXIETY ARE THE SECOND LEADING CAUSE OF DISABILITY IN AUSTRALIA. DEPRESSION IS ON COURSE TO BECOME THE LEADING CAUSE OF DISABILITY *GLOBALLY*.

The impact of stress on mental wellbeing is discussed in Key 7, but it is appropriate to mention here how encouraging regular physical activity in the workplace can help to reduce stress levels and the symptoms associated with anxiety and depression. The costs associated with the loss of work hours, absenteeism, presenteeism, injury and disability, along with the impact on individuals, their work colleagues and their family, are frightening.

Exercise stimulates the release of endorphins that make us feel better and promote a sense of wellbeing. Higher levels of serotonin enable us to better resist negative thoughts and feelings.

It's thought that more active people experience less stress and depression because exercise stimulates the production of norepinephrine. Its role is to modulate the action of other neurotransmitters involved in our response to stress, so it's not just the endorphins that play a role in how well we cope with our everyday stressors.

In a group of people diagnosed with mild to moderate depression, a 12-week course of exercise reduced their symptoms of depression by 47 per cent compared with a group that just did stretching. This improvement was equivalent to that experienced by those prescribed an antidepressant.

It has been estimated that just five minutes of aerobic activity can reduce symptoms of anxiety. If you have a presentation to deliver that's freaking you out, taking time beforehand to go for a jog or brisk walk can make a big difference. Regular exercise can also be very useful for helping ward off feelings of anxiety and depression.

While much of the public focus has been on the escalation of depression in our society, anxiety too can paralyse performance. In the *Stress and wellbeing survey in Australia 2013*, Lyn Casey reported that 28 per cent of Australians experience anxiety, with 12 per cent falling into the severe to extremely severe category.

Anxiety can manifest in the workplace as avoidant behaviour. It activates the stress response and creates a feeling of fear. Concern about meeting deadlines or the expectations of others or our own expectation of performance can put us at risk of increased levels of stress that later manifest as symptoms of anxiety and/or depression.

Exercise has been shown to build resilience to the impact of anxiety on the brain by enabling the hippocampus to regulate the impact of anxiety on the thinking part of the brain, the prefrontal cortex.

Don't stress me out!

A study from Bristol University in 2008 found that those who worked out before work (or in their lunch break) were happier and more resilient and coped better overall. The researchers studied three areas of work performance: mental–interpersonal, output and time demands. Exercise days brought improvement across all three areas. The summary findings included:

» 72 per cent found time management was easier on the exercise days

» 79 per cent reported getting on better with others and feeling well on the days they exercised

» 74 per cent reported finding it easier to cope with their workload.

It also made a difference to levels of stress, motivation and attention. Feeling better about your work is a powerful way to energise your approach to it and get it done. Of course, sometimes the best-laid plans can go awry and there will always be times when our intentions don't work out. Rather than feeling guilty or giving up on the idea altogether, don't stress — because the researchers found that on the days when participants missed an exercise session they maintained a positive mood, reflecting their regular habit, the only deficit being a lower sense of calm.

As with many habits, once the regular routine is established, the benefits continue to accrue despite missing the occasional session. However, while the occasional lapse is insignificant, abandoning a routine altogether quickly negates the benefits of all the hard work you have put in.

Developing a brain-healthy work culture that places a high value on exercise can start by providing all employees with better access to some form of physical activity regime, either at work or somewhere close by, such as a gym or exercise class. If your staff are fitter, happier and more engaged they will be more productive. That has to be good for business.

Tips to boost exercise and physical activity

Getting to and from work

» If you drive to work, look for an alternative option such as cycling or walking. Spending that time walking or cycling can also make the transition between work and home easier.

» Choose to park your car farther away from your destination so you have to walk a bit further.

» If you catch the train, ferry or bus to work, choose to give up your seat and stand for part of your journey. The kind gesture will be good for both parties.

At work

» Schedule in regular brain breaks. Ideally, every 60 to 90 minutes get up and have a 10-minute stretch. Set a timer if necessary as a reminder.

» Choose to stand when on the phone, having a conversation with a colleague or in a meeting.

» Try walking meetings. Rather than meeting up for a coffee, meet for a walk. Walking boosts attention by up to 40 per cent.

» Some companies provide ergonomics, physiotherapy or OT support. Getting someone in to check the height of your workstation, the chair you use and so on can pay big dividends down the track by preventing poor posture, backache, headaches and muscle tension. Instead of a traditional office work chair, how about a wobble chair that keeps your abdominal and back muscles working?

» Incorporate a walk or a jog into your lunch break. If it's a nice day, getting out into the fresh air will really invigorate your mind and help you work better in the afternoon.

» It may be raining, but the gym will be open. A short session can give you that cognitive boost you are looking for.

» Buy a pedometer. They are inexpensive, and an easy way to check in to see how much walking you really do each day.

» Download an app such as Pacer or buy a wearable activity tracker — there are many to choose from, including Fitbit, Jawbone, Nike+ FuelBand and Polar Loop. They are useful as they provide awareness of how active we really are (as opposed to what we believe) and motivate us to reach our target.

Outside work

» Choose an activity that you can engage in three to four times a week. If starting from scratch, check with your doctor first (if over the age of 40) and start with one session of 10 minutes, building intensity and duration from there.

» It's all about fun. If you hate the activity you have chosen, do something else. Remember, gardening, dancing and mowing the lawn all count.

For the organisation

» Lead by example. If the CEO or leader is seen to be physically active, it sends a strong signal that exercise and health matter in this organisation.

» Stand-up meetings are being embraced in the workplace because they have been shown to work more efficiently and be shorter. Everyone stays awake, contributes more and stays more focused on the agenda.

» Set a team challenge. Keep everyone accountable by setting some goals. For example, aim to move four times a day or to sit for one hour less. Having the support and collaboration of coworkers makes it fun and easier to create 'the way we do things around here'.

» Provide information about exercise classes held on and off site. Perhaps offer reduced gym membership fees to staff.

» Allow more flexibility around work hours so staff can incorporate more exercise during their lunch break, for example.

» Hold working lunches outside or in a park with some activities to participate in.

» Provide safe bicycle storage for those who ride to work, and shower facilities for those who exercise before or during work hours.

» Provide ergonomics, physiotherapy or OT support to all staff when they first join the company and as needed during their tenure.

» Encourage all professional development and staff training to incorporate some exercise or physical activity during the day.

» Reward engagement in exercise with incentives, gift vouchers for sports gear or reduced fees for gym membership.

KEY 3
Sleep
Bring me a dream

How many of us as children wouldn't think of sleeping for a hundred years with absolute horror? As far as fairytale fates go, Sleeping Beauty didn't do too badly (no Huntsman on the loose, for example). But in the eyes of a child there can be no worse fate than a seemingly limitless period of enforced inactivity. You could say it's a real ... snooze. But for a busy, working adult, with no time to spare for a day off, let alone an early night? Hand me the spindle, Maleficent. I'll see you in a month or two.

For best brain performance, the one thing never up for negotiation is how much sleep we need.

Full. Stop.

Here's the thing. We spend roughly one-third of our life asleep, yet our understanding of why we sleep, and its relevance to our mood, cognition and wellbeing, is still very young. In a world that often views sleep as a bit of a nuisance, something that stands in the way of our doing other things, knowing why we need sleep is critically important to our high-performance thinking.

Brainy facts on sleep, naptime and working

» Sleep provides us with greater physical and mental wellbeing.

» It allows for neuronal repair and maintenance.

» It brings mood regulation.

» It aids a greater understanding of what we are learning.

» It helps us to consolidate long-term memory.

» It allows us to forget the irrelevant, because we don't need to remember everything forever; sleeping is the time we break those synaptic connections no longer required.

» Sleep makes us more focused and alert.

» We make better decisions and solve problems faster after good-quality sleep.

» It stimulates greater creative and innovative thinking.

» We make fewer mistakes and have fewer accidents when we sleep properly.

» Sleep is the time that the brain clears itself of metabolic waste including amyloid using a unique waste disposal system known as the glymphatic system.

Respect the zeds

Doing with less sleep appears to be another of those little badges of honour that have crept into office culture. For chronic insomniacs who would do almost anything to get just five more minutes' sleep, this has to be the ultimate insult. Why? Because the implication is we're being more disciplined, and in some way superior, if we deliberately cut back on our sleep.

Political leaders such as Winston Churchill and Margaret Thatcher famously got by with only four hours' sleep every night. Good for them, but they are in a very tiny minority of people who can do this and still function normally. Though Winston was perhaps equally famous for his daily naps — more on those later.

SCRAMBLED EGGS AND SLEEP CYCLES

How much sleep is needed to function well will depend on a number of factors, including what animal you are. Humans tend to sleep for anything from five to 11 hours, with the average being seven and three-quarters hours. A cat sleeps for over 12 hours yet a giraffe needs less than two hours. Dolphins are even niftier with their sleep, being able to effectively shut down one hemisphere of their brain at a time so they can stay constantly alert for predators.

Generally we need between seven and eight hours of uninterrupted sleep for maximum restorative and rejuvenating benefit. Each night we experience between four and six sleep cycles, each lasting approximately 90 minutes.

During these cycles we spend some time in what is called deep sleep and some time in what is called REM (rapid eye movement) sleep (see figure 3.1, overleaf). Far from resting, the sleeping brain is highly active, reactivating those neurons that were stimulated during the day, sifting through all the information accumulated, evaluating what we consider is important, and then forming and consolidating our long-term memories.

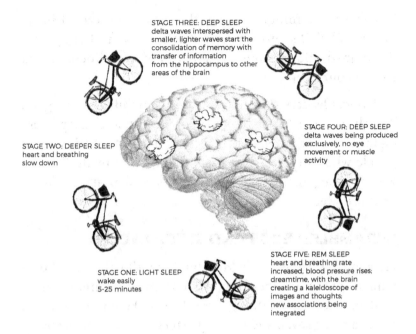

STAGE THREE: DEEP SLEEP
delta waves interspersed with smaller, lighter waves start the consolidation of memory with transfer of information from the hippocampus to other areas of the brain

STAGE FOUR: DEEP SLEEP
delta waves being produced exclusively, no eye movement or muscle activity

STAGE TWO: DEEPER SLEEP
heart and breathing slow down

STAGE ONE: LIGHT SLEEP
wake easily
5-25 minutes

STAGE FIVE: REM SLEEP
heart and breathing rate increased, blood pressure rises; dreamtime, with the brain creating a kaleidoscope of images and thoughts; new associations being integrated

Figure 3.1: the five cycles of sleep (and some sheepish guest stars)

Dreaming is associated mainly with REM sleep. Dreams, or ideas recalled from them, are often credited with inspiring creativity. Paul McCartney based the tune of 'Yesterday' on a dream (for those inclined to get strange things stuck in their heads, the original lyrics involved scambled eggs and lovely legs). Jack Nicklaus attributed an improvement to his golf swing to a dream. The idea for Dr Jekyll and Mr Hyde came to Robert Louis Stevenson in a dream, or would that have been a nightmare?

HOW DO YOU KNOW IF YOU'RE GETTING ENOUGH (SLEEP)?

Your partner may be able to answer this better than you can! If you wake feeling cognitively refreshed, that's a good indication you have had sufficient sleep.

FALLING ASLEEP NORMALLY TAKES BETWEEN FIVE AND 20 MINUTES. IF YOU ARE 'GONE' AS SOON AS YOUR HEAD HITS THE PILLOW, THAT IS AN INDICATION OF EXCESSIVE FATIGUE. IF YOU NEED THREE ALARM CLOCKS TO GET YOU OUT OF BED IN THE MORNING, YOU ARE PROBABLY SLEEP DEPRIVED.

Waking just before your alarm goes off, or not needing an alarm at all, and feeling fresh as a daisy, means you have had enough sleep.

TAKING OUT THE TRASH

Being metabolically highly active, the brain accumulates a lot of waste that needs to be removed. This happens mainly during sleep (well, at least in mice brains!), when our neurons physically shrink to allow our glymphatics, special channels made out of glial cells, to flush out the waste. This process occurs 10 times faster while we sleep than it does in our waking hours.

One concern about sleep deprivation is that it denies the brain its required cleaning time, and may contribute to the acceleration of age-related cognitive decline and neurodegenerative conditions such as Alzheimer's and Parkinson's disease. Maiken Nedergaard likens the system to a fish tank. Keeping the tank clean with a filter is essential to keeping those fish alive.

The same goes for our neurons.

TOO TIRED TO SLEEP

One of the commonest complaints I hear about is a difficulty not so much in falling asleep but in *staying* asleep. Having an over-busy brain can lead to a disturbed sleep pattern with frequent awakenings. The result? We wake up feeling tired, we go to work tired, we come home tired and we are always craving sleep.

With over 96 different recognised sleep disorders to choose from, it's a wonder any of us ever get a good night's sleep.

A SERIES OF BLOWS TO THE COGNITION

The impact of sleep deprivation on our cognition includes:

» a slower response speed

» increased variability of performance

» impaired levels of creativity, innovation and diversity of thought

» impairment of those brain functions more dependent on emotional input, including decision making

» mood disturbance, with higher levels of anxiety and depression

» reduced motivation.

It can take us up to six weeks to recover from one night's lost sleep. Reducing our sleep time to four or five hours a night over as little as one week reduces our cognitive capacity to the equivalent of a blood alcohol level of 0.01 per cent.

WHILE DRUNKENNESS IS NOT TOLERATED IN THE WORKPLACE, EXCESSIVE FATIGUE AND SLEEPINESS IS, EVEN THOUGH THE EFFECT ON OUR COGNITION IS MUCH THE SAME.

People talk about being 'punch-drunk'; one of the literal definitions of this is being dazed and confused from lack of sleep.

Sleep matters to our thinking ability just as much as healthy nutrition and physical exercise. It is a necessity, not a luxury.

Worse still, being sleep deprived causes us to lose the ability to *recognise* that we are tired and cognitively impaired. This is why sleep-deprived drivers continue to drive: their tired brain hasn't told them they need to stop.

I'D DIE TO GO TO SLEEP

Yes, lack of sleep can be deadly.

Fatal Familial Insomnia, while fortunately incredibly rare (known to affect only 40 families around the world), is a genetic prion disease. It manifests in middle age as an increasing inability to fall asleep that leads to death within a few months or several years.

Staying awake for longer has often been seen as a game. Teenagers are the group most likely to pull an all-nighter or stay up partying. Back in 1965, 17-year-old Randy Gardner set out to see if he could set the record for staying awake. He still retains that official record of 11 days and 24 minutes. Others have also attempted to climb the Mount Everest of sleep deprivation, with the National Sleep Research Project claiming an unofficial record of 18 days, 21 hours and 41 minutes.

This is definitely not something to try at home, with side-effects that include hallucinations, paranoia, blurred vision, slurred speech, impaired memory and concentration lapses.

Sleep deprivation is now recognised as a global public health issue. According to the World Association of Sleep Medicine (WASM), sleep problems affect around 45 per cent of the world's population. Thirty per cent of Americans claim they don't sleep well, with between 50 and 70 million people reported as having a sleep or wakefulness disorder:

» 44 per cent reported getting less than seven hours' sleep

» 29 per cent reported either falling asleep or feeling very sleepy while at work

» 12 per cent admitted to having been late for work because of sleep.

The economic burden of the associated presenteeism has been estimated by Kessler and others to be US$63.2 billion.

Similar figures have been collected elsewhere, with the Sleep Health Foundation reporting 13 to 33 per cent of Australians reporting having difficulty either getting to sleep or staying asleep, and studies from Morphy and others revealing 37 per cent of adults in the UK suffer from insomnia.

Sleep cycle expert Charles Czeisler, when asked about the problem of sleeplessness in an interview with the *Harvard Business Review*, advised corporate leaders, 'If you want to raise performance — both your own and your organization's — you need to pay attention to this fundamental biological issue'.

Swing shift

Working too many hours on top of insufficient sleep can lead to an increase in errors and accidents. Some of the world's most catastrophic accidents, including the *Exxon Valdez* oil spill off Alaska, the space shuttle *Challenger* disaster and the Chernobyl nuclear accident, have been linked to sleep deprivation.

When it comes to working excessively long hours, doctors have historically been among the worst culprits. When I worked as a medical intern in the UK in the eighties, it was expected that our work would be hard and challenging, and the hours long.

Very. Long.

For a junior doctor, working what was known as a 1:2 meant being on duty for 36 hours, having one night off and then starting the next 36-hour shift. And we were charged with taking care of others' health!

Once, while driving home in the early-morning rush hour, brain-befuddled after a busy night-shift in the emergency department, I completely ignored a set of traffic lights and drove straight across a busy intersection. I'm not sure who was more horrified — those in the other vehicles or me when I realised what I had done.

I was lucky that time, but how often are workers expected to travel or drive tired?

ACCORDING TO CZEISLER, 20 PER CENT OF ALL MOTOR VEHICLE ACCIDENTS IN THE US ARE DUE TO DRIVER FATIGUE, ACCOUNTING FOR 8000 DEATHS ANNUALLY, WITH 80 000 AMERICANS FALLING ASLEEP AT THE WHEEL.

SLEEPLESS IN SEATTLE, TOKYO, LONDON, SYDNEY ...

Executives are frequently required to travel interstate or overseas for work. Dealing with changes of time zone, navigating around an unfamiliar city, perhaps driving on the other side of the road — all add to the cognitive load on a tired brain.

A company whose work culture accepts sleep deprivation as the norm is putting its employees and its own longevity on the line.

When flying long distances for work, choosing not to travel on red-eye flights and, whenever possible scheduling in an additional day for our body clock to adjust, helps keep our mind clear and our thinking coherent.

Once, sleeping your way to the top had a certain connotation. Today ensuring that all staff, especially those aspiring to climb the corporate ladder, get enough sleep makes very good business sense.

Some people choose to stay awake or work nights:

» for the relative peace and quiet it affords

» because it's part of their job description (emergency workers, FIFO personnel, call centre staff)

» out of simple economic necessity (single-parent families, say, or when the high cost of child care forces a day/night shift arrangement on parents).

How does working nights affect the brain?

Unfortunately, the news is not good. We lose the fine-tuning our circadian rhythm provides to keep us well, even if we are frequent night-shifters. It disrupts up to 97 per cent of those genes that depend on our normal body clock, resulting in increased risk of obesity, type 2 diabetes and heart attack.

Deep in the hypothalamus (the area of the brain concerned with regulating our heart rate, hormone production, body temperature, eating, sleeping and wakefulness), we have a 'sleep ignite' switch, which ties in with our body clock and once initiated allows us to doze off.

Around 1.5 million Australians are currently employed in shift work (equivalent to 16 per cent of the population). In 2013 Shantha Rajaratnam from Monash University published his findings of a review of the health burden associated with shift work.

Here are some of the key points revealed:

» 32 to 36 per cent of shift workers fall asleep at work at least once a week.

» The risk of occupational accidents is at least 60 per cent higher for non-day shift workers.

» Shift workers have higher rates of metabolic and mood disturbances.

» Shift workers have higher levels of inadequate or poor-quality sleep, insomnia and shift work disorder.

With mounting evidence of the risks of sleep deprivation to the health and performance of shift workers, specific advice has been developed for this group of workers based on regular sleep hygiene principles, but tailored for their particular work environment.

I'M SORRY, I CAN'T REMEMBER

Sleep is a highly active process. It's the time when we replay the day's events at high speed, consolidating learning and memory, processing our emotions and restoring homeostasis.

Inadequate sleep unsurprisingly interferes with this process. Worse still, it leads to the formation of false memories. Twenty-four hours of sleep deprivation leads to memory distortion, which is worse if we are already sleep deprived.

Getting enough deep sleep is particularly important for forming memory and is especially relevant for young adults. This starts to lessen with age. By middle age, taking a daytime nap can help us protect our memory, as long as we are getting enough sleep at night.

If you or your staff consistently get less than five hours' sleep at night, the risk of forming false memories is far greater. The ramifications of this include increased potential for human error, miscommunication and misinterpretation. It's a far bigger organisational health risk than simply having tired, grumpy coworkers.

If you have something important to remember or learn, the most effective method is to study the material and then sleep for eight hours. Our memory improves when we are offline.

Sleep myths

Sleep myth #1: You can train yourself to do with less sleep.

Wrong. Next.

(continued)

Sleep myths *(cont'd)*

Sleep myth #2: A nightcap will help you sleep. Hic!

Alcohol definitely hinders rather than helps good sleep. While it may help you feel relaxed and initially get you off to sleep more quickly, the quality of your sleep is reduced. You wake more often during the night and awaken feeling less refreshed. It disrupts the REM part of the sleep cycle, critical to memory retention.

Two alcoholic drinks is enough to halve REM sleep and diminish the amount of time spent in slow wave sleep. This is when memory consolidation occurs with the transfer of information from the hippocampus to other areas of the brain, regulated in part by the medial prefrontal cortex.

Also, alcohol tends to aggravate sleep breathing problems. Sleeping next to a snoring wildebeest does nothing to enhance the relationship and is good for neither the brain nor the chances of continuing connubial bliss.

Sleep stability

You may be the most brilliant ray of sunshine on a normal day, but even the sun can be obscured by clouds when it has been shining non-stop for 48 hours straight. In other words, a lack of sleep can make the most even-tempered person ... snap.

And then there are those grey clouds. They start to turn a very thundery black. Our negativity bias takes over and we start to interpret information differently. We begin to retain only negative thoughts, and even neutral information takes on less of a 'unicorns and rainbows' glow. It's like being permanently wired to an election night special.

FIGHTING SLEEP CAN LEAD TO FISTICUFFS

Why do we find it so hard to turn our frown upside down when we are sleep deprived, and what impact does it have on us in the workplace? Fatigue leads to increased activation of our brain's flight-or-fight system. As we start to panic or punch, our ability to maintain control of our prefrontal cortex, the conscious thinking part of our brain, is diminished.

The brain's brakes — our mental censor of what we should or shouldn't say and do — is located in the PFC. Without access to that, we become more emotionally unstable, likely to lash out, cry, shout, swear or even become physically aggressive.

This isn't fabulous in private, but in the workplace it can have serious consequences, from loss of job to loss of clients or simply loss of face. As a leader, revealing these symptoms makes you vulnerable to a lack of respect from staff; for a staff member, it makes you vulnerable to a lack of trust from your manager, and to derision from your peers.

Prolonged sleep deprivation leads to a build-up of our stress hormones, including cortisol. In excess this is neurotoxic, and in addition contributes to the vicious circle of sleep deprivation leading to impaired cognition and emotion that leads to further sleep disturbance. It can also contribute to abdominal weight gain, which along with the stress leads to — you guessed it — depression and anxiety.

Insomnia and depression have long been linked. Difficulty in sleeping is often an early sign of anxiety and depression, which will in turn increase stress.

PLAYING CATCH-UP DOESN'T WORK

Busy lives and hectic work schedules can lead to sleep being pared back during the week, so we give ourselves the luxury of a weekend lie-in. Sounds good in theory, but it is actually very hard to claw back that sleep debt adequately in just one or two longer sleeps.

It compounds the problem of poor sleep hygiene, and makes it that much harder to get up on time come Monday morning. So try to stay balanced in your sleep times.

STAY AWAY FROM THE (BLUE) LIGHT

Our technology enables us to stay connected with each other and to do our work far beyond the workplace walls. Many people use their smartphone, laptop or tablet to carry on working in the evening, or even during the night. The problem is these technologies emit a blue light that inhibits the production of melatonin, our sleep hormone.

In his book *Night School*, Richard Wiseman reveals that the level of sleep deprivation in the UK is far higher than previously estimated, with 59 per cent of the population in 2014 getting less than the recommended seven hours' sleep a night.

His findings also identified a rapid increase in the proportion of people using their smartphone, computer or tablet at night, from 57 per cent in 2013 to 78 per cent in 2014; and most worryingly, 91 per cent of the 21 to 24 age group.

It's recommended that we switch off from all our devices at least two hours before bedtime, or switch to a device, such as a Kindle, that emits a yellow light that has less effect on the brain.

Also, staying attached to our smartphones or tablets keeps us mentally engaged so we find it harder to switch off to relax and go to sleep. This can contribute to daytime sleepiness.

Sleeping on the job: the power of the nap

Some companies have started looking beyond brain and exercise breaks for tired employees. They have naptime as well.

Why?

Because naps can be highly beneficial to brain function, especially if those brains have been working hard over an extended period of time. Studies by Faraut and others report that a 20-minute nap can increase cognitive performance by up to 40 per cent, with the benefit lasting two to three hours.

In researching the impact of sleep on cognition, NASA looked at the role of naps for pilots on long-haul flights. They discovered that pilots allowed to take a 40-minute nap (on average about 26 minutes of actual sleep) increased their median reaction time by 16 per cent. Pilots not allowed naptime experienced a 34 per cent deterioration in reaction time. More worryingly still, they also experienced an average of 22 micronaps lasting between two and ten seconds during the last 30 minutes of the flight! Overall, NASA found that naps of 26 minutes of sleep led to a 34 per cent increase in cognitive performance and a 54 per cent increase in alertness. Now that's impressive.

One major problem with fatigue is that we lose sight of the fact we are tired. Ignoring those warning signs leads to more errors, wandering attention and loss of vigilance to potential danger.

When overtired, the brain starts to insert microsleeps, thought to be the cause of many motor vehicle accidents. A microsleep is a short period when, while appearing to be awake, we are actually asleep for anything from a fraction of a second to up to half a minute. When we are seriously sleep deprived, some of our neurons will go offline, even while the rest of the brain is awake.

A common time to experience microsleep is when you find yourself sitting in a long and boring meeting and you are already tired. In this situation your brain may simply choose to shut down.

Whether or not your company would benefit from introducing naptime will naturally depend on the type of work being done. Where shift work is the norm or where a lot of creative thought is required, naptime can be a blessing.

It can also depend on the culture of the society as a whole. Siesta has a long tradition in those countries where taking a break during the hottest part of the day to sleep and refuel meant workers could work and stay cognitively fresh longer.

With societal change, globalisation and air conditioning, siesta is now less the norm, replaced in some instances by nap bars. In Barcelona, a chain of nap parlours called *Masajes a 1.000* was set up in 2000 to provide a mini siesta — a five-minute massage and 30-minute nap.

In Japan, where the population sleeps for half an hour less overall than many other countries, organisations such as Toyota and Okuta Corp have incorporated a power-nap system that allows employees to take a 15- to 20-minute nap.

Google and *The Huffington Post* have used sleep pods for a number of years now. The pods themselves look futuristic and have a futuristic price tag to go with them. But you don't need a pod to take a nap, just a quiet space where you can dim the light and not be disturbed. Providing for naptime has resulted in increased productivity and a lower error rate, so it seems the pods will be paying for themselves.

Other US companies such as Ben & Jerry's, Procter & Gamble, Cisco, Zappos and Nike are now classified sleep friendly. One poll found around 6 per cent of US companies now provide employee nap rooms.

Nap room protocols

» Keep the nap short (around 20 minutes) to avoid sleep inertia, that groggy feeling we experience if woken up from a deeper level of sleep.

» Find the right space—somewhere quiet where you won't be disturbed. Close the office door and put a sign up! Keep the room cool and dark or dimly lit.

» While naps can help to prevent workplace sleepiness, this is not about replacing good-quality night-time sleep.

» Keep power naps to the afternoon between lunchtime and no later than 3 pm to avoid disrupting night sleep patterns.

Helping ourselves to sleep better

Like washing our hands to reduce the risk of transmitting illness, good sleep hygiene allows us to enjoy good-quality, uninterrupted sleep so as to wake refreshed, reinvigorated and ready to face our day.

Brainy tips for better sleep hygiene

» Whenever possible keep to a regular 40-minute pre-bed routine to prepare your brain for sleep.

» Unplug from all technology at least two hours before going to sleep, or use a device that emits a yellow light, as found on Kindle. If you use your smartphone as an alarm clock, be sure to turn off the display screen and the ringer to avoid being disturbed by incoming texts and messages.

» Keep to a regular getting-up time and avoid the temptation to sleep in. If necessary, go to bed 20 to 30 minutes earlier when you need to catch up.

» Keep the bedroom for sex and sleeping only.

» Maintain the room temperature at around 19 degrees Celsius, and keep the room dark and quiet.

» Avoid putting a sheet under the doona; it affects the quilt's 'breathability'.

» Choose your sleeping partners carefully — and that includes the dog!

» If you or your partner snore (a lot) get a check-up to find out whether you have a sleep disorder such as sleep apnoea.

» Avoid sleep poison: caffeine, alcohol, smoking and big meals at bedtime.

» Complete any exercise two to three hours before bedtime.

» Avoid napping other than a power nap during the day (preferably before 3 pm) to avoid interfering with normal sleep patterns.

» If stress or a mood disorder is making it harder for you to sleep, try a relaxation technique such as mindfulness or another form of meditation.

» If chronic lack of sleep is affecting your performance, relationships or wellbeing, see your doctor.

Brainy tips for avoiding workplace fatigue

» Lead by example. If the CEO or manager is shown to value rest and sleep as good work hygiene, others will follow.

» Discussion, education and documentation are needed when granting permission to sleep or take a nap for the sake of work safety and productivity.

» Educate staff about good sleep hygiene and the roles of caffeine, alcohol and switching off from technology early enough.

» To minimise fatigue, provide a workplace environment that is bright, well lit and ventilated, and a comfortable temperature.

» Identify where fatigue may be a hazard in the workplace and assess the risk.

» Adopt a risk management approach.

» Limit total working hours per week.

» Arrange rosters so everyone gets at least one day off each week.

» If your staff don't need to be working after hours, consider limiting access to the internal server at night.

» Provide facilities on site for people to take a work break or a nap.

» Provide on-site sleeping accommodation for staff where necessary.

» Design shift-work times to minimise the impact of fatigue and if necessary stipulate the required down time.

» Devise procedures for those areas where staff are performing safety-critical tasks or working in harsh environments to ensure regular breaks are taken and safety procedures followed.

KEY 4
Mental stretch
Flexing our mental muscles

Think back to when you were a child. Remember that curiosity that drove you to explore everything within reach, to want to go on voyages, take on quests and slay the dragon? Like the boy who eventually became King Arthur in the classic tale *The Sword In the Stone*, during our lifetime we will have incredible experiences. Perhaps we won't have Merlin at our side, but we have our own source of magic: a massively plastic brain with the capacity to learn new skills and form memory and thought processes.

By sustaining that sense of wonder and adventure from our childhood in our adult years, staying curious allows us to develop a stronger and more resilient brain, with the mental muscles needed to avoid rapid cognitive decline.

We reach our cognitive peak in our early twenties, but it is our conscious decision to remain engaged and interested in what the world has to offer as we age that, like actively brushing and flossing our teeth and gums, prevents brain decay.

**THE MORE WE USE OUR BRAIN,
THE BETTER IT GETS.**

Those who choose to stretch their minds will be the ones who adapt more readily, innovate more and engage in possibility thinking. They will be our Once and Future Brain Kings (and Queens).

Brainy facts about neuroplasticity and business

» Neuroplasticity is the brain's ability to form new connections between existing neurons. These connections, called synapses (see figure 4.1), develop as a consequence of everything we learn, store and remember. So the more you drive your brain's plasticity, the better your ability to function at a high level in meetings, while delivering workshops or mentoring — the list goes on. Why? Because if you have a high level of neuroplasticity, it means you are constantly seeking out new information and expanding your repertoire of knowledge and understanding — and you will also be retaining more, because we remember more of what we are interested in.

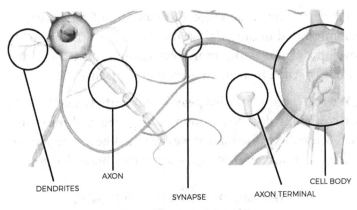

DENDRITES

AXON

SYNAPSE

AXON TERMINAL

CELL BODY

Figure 4.1: synapses at work

» You may have agonised over your first few clumsy efforts to drive a car or to play a recognisable tune on a musical instrument, but with practice the associated neural pathways were strengthened and accessed more quickly. This allowed you to perform these tasks more easily, until they became 'automatic', no longer requiring conscious thought. Hebb's rule states that 'neurons that fire together wire together'. This means once you have acquired a new skill, it quickly becomes hardwired into your synapses.

» Our brain's plasticity leads us to smarter thinking. Win–win.

» As this is a natural biological phenomenon, we don't have to do anything for it to happen. However, we can drive our plasticity to our advantage through our choice of focus.

» It's less about boosting intelligence per se than about how we use the information already available to us. It provides us with the means to be:

  » more adaptive

  » more focused

  » more insightful

  » more agile in dealing with a mountain of data

  » more innovative

  » more adept in managing emotion

  » more sensitive to social and cultural differences

  » more collaborative.

What we focus on changes our brain, and this is what gives us our cognitive advantage.

Curiosity breeds success

As sociobiologist Desmond Morris noted, 'We never stop investigating. We are never satisfied that we know enough to get by', and during the course of our evolution, it has been our natural curiosity that has fostered learning by capturing our attention. What interests us determines our focus, and what we learn and will remember. Our pursuit of new information rewards our brain with the release of dopamine that drives us to continue in our quest. Also, we use our working memory in the prefrontal cortex to help us distinguish something that is new from something we have encountered already (although as we age our capacity to make this distinction can sometimes go a bit awry!).

One of the common traits of those who live the longest on the planet (while remaining cognitively intact) is their continuing curiosity about what is going on around them — their active engagement with the world.

THE MORE CURIOUS WE REMAIN, THE MORE WE STIMULATE OUR BRAIN PLASTICITY.

WHEN I WAS A CHILD, I THOUGHT AS A CHILD

Our brain shrinks with age, around 2 per cent per decade. Increasing the brain's plasticity and neurogenesis can help to keep us mentally sharp and retain the cognitive edge we need in life — and especially in work, as the retirement age stretches closer to our eighth decade.

It used to be thought that the brain was hardwired, and we had only a short period of relative plasticity in our early childhood that allowed us to learn complex tasks — for example, a second language. Wrong! We never stop learning or adjusting to change in our environment. Although our brain's plasticity does decline with age, which means it takes more effort to learn new skills, we don't lose it completely, so there is always the potential to boost how well we think.

Glenn Capelli, the author of *Thinking Caps*, reminds us that maintaining a childlike curiosity helps us to absorb new ideas and ways of doing things. *Neoteny* means the retention of juvenile characteristics, implying a delay in our physiological development. Capelli believes we can apply neoteny to our thinking, thereby by preserving a child's spontaneity, creativity, love of exploration and living with a sense of wonder.

It's why:

» we are absorbed by the worlds we discover when watching Professor Brian Cox or David Attenborough on TV

» we choose to read fiction and lose ourselves in stories

» we are easily distracted by articles we find while surfing the net; the information may not be relevant to us right now, but it adds to our repertoire and may be useful to us later.

We may chide ourselves for 'time wasting', yet all these pursuits are actually hugely important for our mental muscles. They can lead us towards that state of flow, as described by Mihaly Csikszentmihalyi, in which we find ourselves immersed in building knowledge and competence. And knowledge and competence are, of course, essential in our business lives, stimulating a healthy, fit business brain and future proofing our ability to succeed in our commercial realm.

BRIGHT SPARKS

Cultivating curiosity begins with the need to know. A person who is curious and open to discovery doesn't accept that our 'best' will still be our best tomorrow.

BEING CURIOUS IS HOW WE STRETCH OUR MIND TOWARDS NEW IDEAS AND DISCOVERIES. IF WE ARE INTERESTED IN A SUBJECT, A PERSON OR AN IDEA, THEN KEY LEARNINGS FROM THEM WILL FLOW – AND FEEL EASY AND EFFORTLESS.

CULTIVATING CURIOSITY

As a kid, Jack Andraka seemed to be no different from his mates, except he came from a scientific family who had always spent time sitting around the dinner table together talking about world issues and reading books.

When a family friend died from pancreatic cancer, Jack became aware of, and curious about, the difficulty of early diagnosis. What could be done differently to help improve the woeful prognosis of this dreadful disease? The idea he came up with was a simple, inexpensive dipstick test for use on blood and urine to detect a biomarker in the early stage of the disease.

Jack's idea won him the Intel Gordon E. Moore Award in 2012, at the tender age of 15.

Impressive? Absolutely. It takes a burning desire for knowledge to seek answers to unsolved mysteries. While Jack's idea remains to be validated by scientific publication, clinical trials and further research, his story is about setting out to discover 'why can't we improve this'. When we are curious, we stop focusing on what we already know and instead focus on finding out 'what else?'

So how curious are you? Do you enjoy learning new things or would you rather just get on with what you feel comfortable with? Does the thought of being sent to work in an unknown land excite you, or put you in a tailspin of anxiety and horror that you might be expected to eat stuff you wouldn't recognise as food or have to converse with people whose language you don't understand? If you are presented with a new gadget, are you curious about how it works or do you simply want to know where the on/off switch is?

We actually know relatively little about what curiosity is and how it works. A study by Charan Ranganath and Matthias Gruger set out to discover why we remember certain things and not others and how we can make learning the really boring stuff a bit easier.

Have you ever wondered why some people seem to have a knack for remembering those snippets of information that most of us would have absolutely no use for in our daily lives? While remembering who won the baseball World Series in 2012 or the cumulative age of the Rolling Stones might be useful for playing Trivial Pursuit or on quiz nights, it turns out our curiosity activates certain brain areas, as recorded on brain scans, and rewards us with some extra dopamine.

This helps us with remembering the minutiae and boring stuff too. When we are being curious about what happens in the finale of our favourite TV series, for example, we are more likely to remember things like where we were and who we were with when we watched it. This creates a higher level of other associations, which while not directly linked to the subject matter, makes it easier for the brain to remember that you were sitting next to Susan on the sofa and she was wearing a red shirt.

THE MORE CURIOUS WE ARE ABOUT OUR WORLD, THE MORE OPEN WE ARE TO LEARNING AND REMEMBERING OTHER THINGS AS WELL.

As Robert Bilder says, 'curiosity enhances learning'. This is crucial in the workplace, because it means we can use our curiosity to deepen and extend our area of expertise, which sets us up to broaden our retention of knowledge in other areas as well.

Train your brain to change your mind

Sometimes when asked what I do, I'll explain how I teach people to become more brain fit to optimise their mental performance. The most common response to this is, 'Oh, it's like those computer brain games is it?'

Online brain training programs are increasing in popularity, but on their own they are no panacea for growing a stronger, more resilient brain. Digital brain training programs put together under the guidance of neuroscientists and neuropsychologists do have their merits, but we can easily challenge our brain using other low-cost, low-tech methods.

This can be as easy as doing a cryptic crossword or learning how to juggle or dance a tango. These types of activities are useful for mental stretch because they provide us a smorgasbord of new tasks and functions to learn, and variance in the way in which we use our neural pathways.

The benefit of the online programs is their accessibility and how enticing they are, with their promise of improving your reaction speed, spatial awareness and memory. If spending 10 to 15 minutes a day on these programs appeals, then do it. However, if you have the choice between staying in and working on the computer or going out to watch a play, catch a movie or have dinner with friends, the latter options are far superior in driving your brain's plasticity.

Does brain training work? That depends on what you mean by brain training, and whom you ask!

Brain training is as it sounds. It is training designed to improve specific brain functions. Many brain games and apps on the market provide great entertainment, but they do not necessarily lead to a neurobiological change resulting in effective and enduring improvement in brain function.

By practising different skillsets, we become more efficient and faster when performing tasks within a game. But does this actually translate into an increase in functionality as we go about our lives, or improve our business capability?

In 2015 Megan Spencer-Smith and Torkel Klingberg undertook a systematic review and meta-analysis of working memory training programs that showed a statistically significant benefit in reducing inattention in daily life. This is promising in view of the large number of children and adults who have difficulties with attention and focus. (It must be mentioned that Klingberg perhaps has a vested interest, in that he put together the Cogmed working memory program.)

Other researchers are not convinced. Monica Melby-Lervag and Charles Hume from Oslo failed to show any transfer of effect in their meta-analysis published in 2012.

So what does this mean? That a good dose of healthy scepticism remains in order until such time as more evidence is available to us. Meanwhile, if you enjoy these games, carry on — just don't expect a miracle. As our understanding of the brain continues to expand, there will probably come a time, sooner rather than later, when we can be confident that our training is producing the desired effect: positive and enduring changes in brain function and performance.

The authors of *The SharpBrains Guide to Brain Fitness: How to Optimize Brain Health and Performance at Any Age* are careful to outline the conditions under which brain training can work.

The training must:

» 'engage and exercise a core brain-based capacity or neural circuit identified to be relevant to real-life outcomes

» target a performance bottleneck

» be a minimum of 15 hours total per targeted brain function

» adapt to performance, require effortful attention and increase in difficulty.'

If I only had a brain: the Tin Man and other brainy myths

Before moving on to how to create more daily difference, there are a couple of myths to dispel.

MYTH #1: WE USE ONLY 10 PER CENT OF OUR BRAIN

This is, in a nutshell, inherently wrong and diminishes how amazing the human brain really is. We use *all* of our brain, *most* of the time. It would be very wasteful not to!

A child born congenitally blind still has the brain space allocated for the interpretation of visual stimuli, but it will be used instead for different purposes.

When an area of brain tissue is damaged by injury, the brain will recruit other areas to take over the lost function. This understanding on its own has revolutionised the medical approach to the management of stroke.

Previously a person who had sustained a brain injury through stroke would be offered six months of treatment to assist in the recovery of function. It was believed (wrongly) that that was the physiological limit of what could be expected. Today we understand better that the biological process of recovery takes a long time and can be painfully slow.

Jill Bolte Taylor, author and neuroanatomist from Harvard, had a massive stroke at the age of 37 that wiped out much of her left hemisphere. Her background meant she knew she could use her brain's plasticity to help her recover. When she realised what was happening to her, she remembered thinking, 'I'm a very busy woman, I don't have time for a stroke! So I'll do this for a week or two, and then I'll get back to my routine'.

It took a little bit longer than a week or two. Eight long years to relearn how to walk, talk, read and write. Her TED talk 'My Stroke of Insight' is a remarkable testament to the power of the human mind.

MYTH #2: WE ARE EITHER RIGHT BRAINED OR LEFT BRAINED

Neither. We are both.

We are born with two hemispheres joined together by a thick band of *corpus callosum*, and they communicate with each other all the time. While each side may have some difference in function, we use whole-brain thinking. Labelling ourselves as left brained or right brained does us (and our brains) a disservice.

Remember, it's all about where we choose to place our focus. If you are fascinated by science you may spend your days looking at data, but you can still appreciate music and art. If you are more artistically inclined, you may also be interested in maths and how robots can help our lives.

MYTH #3: BRAIN TRAINING MAKES YOUR BRAIN YOUNGER

Sorry to disappoint, but training it isn't going to change the age of your brain. It's not like plastic surgery where we try to make ourselves look younger than we are. What it can do is enhance certain aspects of how well we use parts of our brain. It's better to think of the training as polishing up those areas we pay more attention to.

Overall, your brain will continue to age along with the rest of you. Some processes, such as learning new skills, do slow down as we age; however, in turn we gain wisdom and studies suggest we are less stressed by extraneous circumstances. Stress does contribute to the aging process in terms of how well our brain works.

MYTH #4: BRAIN TRAINING DOESN'T WORK

The first 'brain games' on the market offered little more than entertainment. The challenge has been to provide evidence that brain training produces not just improvement in the programs themselves through effort and practice, but real, enduring, positive change applicable to real life.

If you are considering trialling a brain training program, ask intelligent and forthright questions upfront. What does this program purport to do? How will it make a difference to me? Is it set up in such a way that I can ascertain how well I am currently performing in a specific task? Does it allow me to monitor my progress? How will this training translate into real benefits in the world I live in?

An athlete preparing to improve their physical fitness will often target certain areas of muscle in addition to general fitness work. A golfer may target their swing. A sprinter may focus on their start. In the same way, when choosing a brain training program it's important to know which of your mental muscles you want to focus on and the best technique to achieve that.

Participating in short bursts of brain training isn't enough. Ideally it's about committing to a minimum of 15 hours over eight weeks — and that is a minimum.

If you joined a gym but turned up only once or twice a month you wouldn't expect to see the same level of improvement in your level of physical fitness compared with committing to two or three sessions a week. To get the most benefit out of a brain training program you need to spend three or four 45-minute sessions each week. Some programs recommend continuing for three months, with occasional 'top-ups' thereafter.

Take the challenge: could you pull the sword from the stone?

The challenge of creating a daily habit of difference is to step out of our comfort zones, to try something new, something different, something we may not be very good at. It's about making our brain more muscular so we are at our best when we need to be — in the workplace.

I am not talking about being *the* best. I'm talking about being *your* best. To go back to our childhood stories, when 'the Wart' pulled the sword out of the stone to become 'the true and rightful King of all England', it wasn't because he thought he was the most fabulous thing since silver chainmail. It was because he was attempting to do his job as a squire properly.

So flexing your mental muscles is less about being 'the best' and more about stimulating your brain to be 'your best' to create new synaptic connections, putting in the necessary practice to strengthen them and continuing with the challenge. This is because once you have mastered a new skill, unless you continue to push the boundaries of your competence, the benefit of the challenge starts to diminish.

In starting any new challenge the three core components are:

» *novelty*. Take on something your brain doesn't recognise or hasn't done before.

» *variety*. Try a smorgasbord of different things.

» *continuing challenge*. The challenge doesn't stop with mastery of the first level; that's just to get you started!

Brain time at the gym for the individual

Start with one small change at a time

» If you have always wanted to learn a musical instrument, or to dance or paint, it's time to sign up for the class.

» If not now, when?

Make it a daily habit

» Do a cryptic crossword.

» Learn three new words and their meanings.

» Read a book in a different genre from your common preference.

» Learn and recite a poem.

Ditch the props

» Navigate using your inner compass. Leave behind that list of items you need from Officeworks and challenge your brain to remember them.

Chase up old flames

» Pick a song from your past and recall the artist and the year it was released.

» Still got that clarinet tucked away in a cupboard? You may not have played it for a while, but why not rediscover your former talent and look to take it to the next level?

Brain time at the gym for the workplace

Develop a culture of curiosity

Encourage self-reflection around performance.

» What do people see themselves doing well?

» Ask what could be done differently to get a better outcome.

» A curious leader may reflect on how well they are leading others.

» Encourage acceptance of a diversity of perspective. This draws people together to share ideas and consider other ways of doing things.

Change the language

» Eliminate knowing and replace it with questioning ('What could we be doing better?').

» Choose to move from 'what is' to 'what if?'

Change the mode of thinking

» Have a reason to expand thinking that's meaningful to the person and use a different way to explore the new territory. This could be using a more 'gameful' approach, using riddles and puzzles and encouraging group participation.

Part II
Operating a high-performance brain

KEY 5
Focus
Adjusting our lens
of attention

Imagine. It's World War I. You are an officer in the British Army; not a cushy, General Sir Hogmanay Melchett in *Blackadder* sort of officer. No Sah. You are in the trenches with your men, just another fellow in the 6th Battalion, Royal Scots Fusiliers, although you do have a bit of a propensity for danger missions into no man's land.

Now you are sitting there in the trenches on the front in Ploegsteert, Belgium. Unlike most of the waterlogged, rat-infested bogholes that make up the front line, the 6th's trenches have a remarkable lack of one thing. *Lice.* That's because you are Lieutenant Colonel Churchill, later Prime Minister Sir Winston Churchill, and the first thing you did as commander of the battalion was recognise the need to de-louse your men so they aren't distracted from the task at hand.

The ability to focus on what really matters, and to do it quickly and confidently, is seen as one of most essential attributes for success in the modern business arena. But this tells only half the story. What matters more is our ability to ignore the multitude of distractions that work to pull us away from the task at hand. As Sir Winston said, 'You will never reach your destination if you stop and throw stones at every dog that barks'.

We need to be able not only to focus, but to fix that focus and narrow it to an attention span that remains constant and unwavering.

Our ability to pay attention is a survival tool that the brain developed as a means of keeping us safe, fed and sheltered. Without attention, we cannot learn. If we do not learn, we do not encode memory. If we lack memory, we have nothing to add to our life store of experience. What we have experience in influences what we direct our attention to and make a success of, and therefore earn a living at, which takes us back to being safe, fed and sheltered.

Bottom line: Attention matters for performance.

Brainy facts about our attention span and work

» The neurophysiology of attention is highly complex, but the basic premises include the following:

 » Attention shapes the brain.

 » Attention, being a highly energetic process, is designed to be used for short chunks of time to be effective.

 » If we don't consciously choose to give it a break, the brain instigates its own attention breaks (mind wandering).

» The prefrontal cortex works to synchronise all our sensory systems to enable us to focus our attention.

» Paying attention leads to the formation of new neural circuits or pathways. As these circuits get bigger, bands of gamma brainwave activity start to run across the brain, essentially binding separate brain regions together.

» We have three attentional networks (see figure 5.1, overleaf):

» alerting

» orientating

» executive.

The alerting network implies that, yes, we have to be awake to pay attention. Our level of alertness influences the amount of attention paid. When we first wake up, it takes several minutes for our brains to start registering what is going on around us. We rely a lot on the visual stimuli we receive via our environment to determine what we choose to focus our attention on.

The orientating network refers to how we orientate ourselves to the process, using our eyes to look, our ears to listen, and other senses including touch, taste and smell.

The executive network is the prefrontal cortex, including the anterior cingulate, which is related to the dopamine network. Here we use conscious thought to direct our actions so they are aligned to our goals.

(continued)

Brainy facts about our attention span and work *(cont'd)*

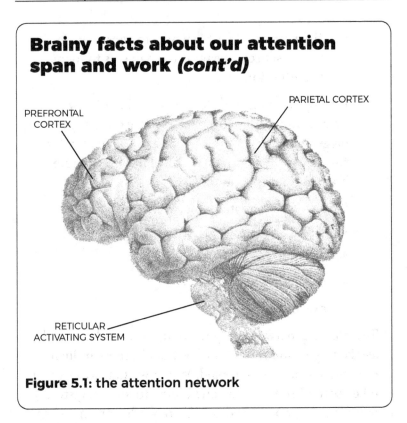

PARIETAL CORTEX

PREFRONTAL CORTEX

RETICULAR ACTIVATING SYSTEM

Figure 5.1: the attention network

Fragmented focus

Our ability to pay attention is highly complex and fragile. Think about what happens when you sit down at your desk. You start work diligently enough, but within five minutes distraction sets in, because someone sends you something interesting via LinkedIn, or you notice a message from a friend in your inbox, or you decide to sneak a look at the latest issue of *Gourmet Traveller* on your iPad.

We have the ability to find information to complete a task with the click of a web tab, but the challenge most of us face every day is not how focused we are but how very easily we are distracted.

It has been argued that our attention span is shrinking rapidly as a consequence of our inability to manage our distractions; and that our technology is designed to add to this, rather than aid our focus. This is of major concern for these main reasons:

» We think in sound bites without developing the full story.

» We surface-skim information and as a result fail to develop a deeper understanding of what we actually need to know.

» Fragmenting our time and our attention makes us less efficient.

» Distractions put us at risk of making more mistakes or of accidents, particularly in the workplace or on the way to and from the workplace.

» Relationships, both personal and professional, are damaged through insufficient attention.

Developing our intelligence around how we pay attention to our tasks and to others is key to allowing us to:

» maintain our cognitive energy across our day

» learn effectively

» form memory and develop new skills

» recall information at the appropriate time

» reduce errors and stay safe

» maintain relationships.

Give your brain a break

Despite our best intentions in terms of our attitude and theoretical desire to focus, distraction will occur. For example, how well can you concentrate when you are hungry, tired, sleep deprived, too cold or hot, feeling unwell, on medication (especially those that helpfully warn they may cause drowsiness), in a noisy environment, being distracted or procrastinating?

WE HAVE TO MANAGE OUR COGNITIVE ENERGY.

Busy days and long hours take their toll on our thinking and performance.

Creating a healthy brain by integrating the healthy lifestyle choices described in the earlier keys will help provide us with the mental energy we need to get through our day. Tony Schwartz, CEO of the Energy Project, recommends we act as our own chief energy officer to monitor when we need a 'rest and refuel' stop.

Whatever our work practice or schedule, our brain is designed to work in roughly the same way: in chunks of time following the natural flow of peaks and troughs of our energy. This is known as our ultradian rhythm (see figure 5.2). Discovered by Nathan Kleitman, this 90-minute cycle of energy takes us through different levels of alertness; remember that alertness is one of the key networks for attention. By choosing to work in sync with this natural flow of energy we can increase our productivity and efficiency by limiting our periods of focus.

Working to a deadline within this framework can also give us that extra oomph to focus our attention and complete a focused task, because we have the welcome reward of a break, such as a nice cup of tea, to look forward to.

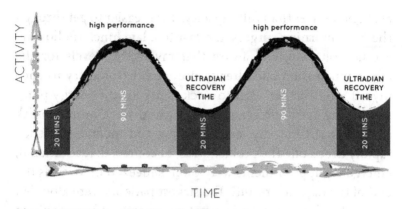

Figure 5.2: the ultradian rhythm

It's like interval training in exercise. Running for 20 kilometres can be a slog. Running for four kilometres then taking a break before continuing will get you to the same destination, but feeling less tired overall. Well, that's the theory!

YOUR BRAIN IS A 100-METRE SPRINTER, NOT TENZING NORGAY.

When my husband and I climbed Mt Kinabalu, the second day of the climb started around 3 am so we could reach the summit before sunrise. We were very excited and keen to get going, but our guide, who was very wise, advised us to 'tread slowly, tread slowly'. He made us stop frequently to catch our breath. And he was right. We passed a number of other people determined to be first to the summit, but by starting too fast and going for too long in the high altitude, they ran out of energy. Slow and steady with plenty of breaks got us to our destination in time to witness the splendid sight of the first rays of sunlight kissing the tops of the adjacent mountains.

The same principle applied when I was working in my medical practice. Most days were big days so I would try to pace myself, a bit like a jogger in a long-distance run. By starting off at slightly lower than full capacity, it was easier to get through the busy morning surgery and last to a late lunch. Following a quick pit stop, and aware that my energy levels for the afternoon session had already dropped, I would try to pace myself a bit further. Four o'clock is my lowest energy point for the day. If I don't get a cup of tea and a five-minute break around that time, my level of focus and mental efficiency rapidly drops off. The problem was, of course, that additional, emergency appointments were often squeezed in towards the end of the day. The result? The sickest patients were attended to by a tired doctor who was not necessarily at her cognitive freshest or best.

Pacing your day in chunks of focused thinking time, interspersed with 'brain out' breaks, means your brain can operate more efficiently. You remain more alert and attentive, which means fewer mistakes and a chance to finish on time.

BY WORKING WITH YOUR BRAIN'S NATURAL DESIGN YOU WORK LESS TO GET MORE DONE, AND DONE WELL. EFFICIENCY AND A CUP OF TEA – WHO COULD ASK FOR MORE?

Many workplaces have now become completely immersed in the cultural expectation of continual performance that seemed to rise to prevalence in the late eighties. Now that we are aware that this actually drives performance down, how can you manage your cognitive energy to work with your brain's natural energy cycle within this environment?

Does your workplace value longer working hours in the mistaken belief that this leads to increased productivity?

Is overtime expected as a means to keep up with the amount of work that has to be done?

Staying late to finish an important task will occasionally be necessary, but simply working longer because your boss expects you to demonstrate your commitment has been shown to be counterproductive, as we simply expand our work to fit the greater time available. It was Bob Pozen, author of *Extreme Productivity*, who said, 'Time becomes an easy metric to measure how productive someone is, even though it doesn't have any necessary connection to what they achieve'.

You don't pay attention to me anymore

'Attention is the rarest and purest form of generosity.'
Simone Weil

We're not very generous with our attention anymore, and when we receive it we rarely recognise what a gift we are given: it allows us to connect at a far deeper level; it builds trust, relatedness and understanding.

Can you remember the last conversation you had where the other person gave you their complete and undivided attention? How did it make you feel?

Active listening is a leadership skill that can dramatically improve interpersonal relationships. Too often we spend our conversations playing ping-pong in our own heads, composing our response before we've given the other person a chance to finish. Leaders who listen more and speak less are more effective communicators. It is the clarity of message that matters, and that comes from fully assimilating all the information provided.

In negotiations and dispute resolution, ensuring that each side is fully heard allows progress to be made more quickly and means both sides are more likely to consider a compromise. It puts the brain in a more relaxed state, reducing the emotional component of the discussion, and keeps the thinking part of our brain (the prefrontal cortex) more accessible.

Our current mental disposition has been described as a state of continuous partial attention. This keeps the brain in a state of high alert, which is not only exhausting but restricts our ability to stay on task and relate with others. In his book *Focus: The Hidden Driver of Excellence*, Daniel Goleman describes how this continuous partial attention is diminishing our ability to form rapport or to engage at a deeper level, because this requires a shared focus between two people.

Perhaps you have noticed how hard it is to hold on to the thread of a conversation if you're busy sorting out paperwork, attending to an urgent email and checking your diary for your next appointment — all at the same time.

In a 2005 paper for *Harvard Business Review*, 'Overloaded circuits: why smart people underperform', psychiatrist Ned Hallowell revealed a new phenomenon, a psychological condition he was seeing with increasing frequency. This condition was causing those affected to lose their sense of perspective, to suffer a high level of distractibility and a variety of psychosomatic complaints such as fatigue, insomnia, mental stress, anxiety, panic and guilt. For many people the condition he called Attention Deficit Trait (ADT) has become the 'norm'.

This condition was noted to be remarkably similar to Attention Deficit Disorder (ADD), which affects between 4 and 5 per cent of adults. If you recognise these tendencies in yourself (or perhaps your partner), remember that your inability to function with clarity and focus could be explained by ADT rather than ADD.

It's important to differentiate between the two. The main difference is that ADT is *purely* the result of the environment we create and live in. As our lives have become increasingly complex and our work more demanding, our brain sometimes responds by going into survival mode — and that means our thinking capacity shrinks.

CEOs and managers, being high achievers, are especially at risk. Being good at focusing, prioritising and managing challenges, they will often have worked out a series of strategies to deal with their workload; except, as the hamster wheel of work spins ever faster, the time spent trying not to fall off increases. As fatigue kicks in, our ability to stay focused on the bigger picture is reduced and we start behaving in a reactive way, putting out continual spot fires, which only exacerbates the situation.

Managing ADT starts with understanding how the brain responds to stress and how our high levels of distractibility reduce our ability to manage our fragmented attention. Then it's about putting in place a program to create the ideal work environment in which the brain feels safe and can perform at its very best.

CEOs have shared with me a number of strategies that they have found helpful.

CEO v ADT: the TKO

Providing your brain with regular breathing space to think

This might mean closing the office door, unplugging from our technology or changing the place where we work.

Working with your distractions

It can be tempting to see distractions as a uniquely modern nuisance, though the reality is they have always been there. What has changed is the volume of distractions we now have to deal with and our perception that they are ruling our lives.

(continued)

CEO v ADT: the TKO *(cont'd)*

The human brain is constantly evolving to adapt to our rapidly changing environment. Berating ourselves for our lack of attention and high distractibility is unhelpful and unnecessary, because we can rebuild our attention and learn to take control of our distractions.

Distractions are part and parcel of everyday life; they are not going to go away. The new strategy is to work with them rather than against them.

Managing straws and camels

It's not the first interruption that drives us batty, or the second or the third. It's that final tipping point, which can be tiny and trivial, the arrival of *just one more thing* that catapults us into the zone of overload, frustration, anger or despair.

Our emotional reaction to frustration reduces our productivity further. Getting annoyed or cross might not be an unusual response, but it costs us additional focus time.

We can reduce the stress response by choosing to manage our emotional state effectively. Better still, we need only the *perception* of having a handle on our emotions to regain cognitive control. In other words, fake it ... until you retake it.

Our CEO of Distraction Pty Ltd

The board members of the Distraction Corporation (distraction.com. It's a state of ... oooooh, what's that? Shiny!) are readily identifiable. Email, phone calls, meetings, text messages and people.

However, the CEO of all our distractions is the one we commonly overlook even though it is in plain sight.

Us. You. Me. Boss 'Checking Facebook While I Pretend To Listen To This Phone Call And Finish This White Paper' Us.

According to a study in *Science* by Killingsworth and Gilbert, we distract ourselves 46.9 per cent of the time. The only time we don't distract ourselves is while making love. (Though there is now some disturbing new evidence that those pesky external distractors, our mobile phones, are encroaching on even this sacred time, with 62 per cent of women and 48 per cent of men admitting to checking their mobile phones during sex!)

So what are we doing when we distract ourselves?

We are either planning our future or ruminating about our past, which doesn't leave much time to get on with the task in front of us right now. This is now such a major problem for high-performance thinkers that the next chapter is devoted to how to get our brain to stay in the here and now.

Rage against the machines?

Is our modern technology really bad for our brains?

It would seem that in relation to our ability to pay attention the answer is yes. While few would prefer to go back to a world before mobile phones or the interwebs, we have paid for these modern conveniences with a vastly reduced attention span, and this is changing our brain.

Daniel Levitin, author of *The Organised Mind*, compares our smartphones to the Swiss army knives beloved by previous generations of young boys. Our phones are not 'phones'. They are powerful processors that allow us to send texts, check our email, take photographs, play games and update our social media. We make restaurant bookings; buy clothes; book airline tickets, hotels and cruises; update our diary; have face-to-face business meetings; find the nearest bottle shop; do our grocery shopping; and make doctor's appointments.

Sometimes we even make a phone call.

Their portability and ease of use have made smartphones a worldwide phenomenon. They have now overtaken desktop computers as our first form of new technology (54 per cent to 46 per cent). The level of connectivity and accessibility they provide has contributed to our rapid globalisation.

The dark side of all this is the level of distractibility and addictive potential that is seemingly built into every app. We use these tools to pack every waking moment. While commuting to and from work we play music or games or check our phone messages. On buses, trams, trains and pavements the parade of the 'heads down tribe', as they have become known in China, now dominates our social settings. People are in essence spending time together but are no longer communicating in person, except via text or tweet.

Some scientists, such as Barbara Fredrickson, are concerned that our passion for social media is compromising our biological ability to connect with other people. Digital natives interact via arcane redacted text language instead of face-to-face conversations in real time. Many are finding it hard to cope with 'personal' conversations or when they have to confront someone with a work issue or discuss problems — or, even harder, real emotions. This loss of resilience and coping skills is manifesting in increasing levels of anxiety, especially in the under-25 age group. This impacts social cohesiveness and therefore commercial collaborative ability and engagement. We've probably all experienced being 'phubbed' occasionally — that social snub by the person we're with who chooses to engage with their mobile phone instead of engaging in conversation with you. It feels disrespectful and can seriously damage that relationship.

Sheri Turkle, author of *Together Alone*, says unless we can learn to be alone with our imagination, we will only ever know how to be lonely. Maggie Jackson, in her book *Distracted*, takes this one step further, believing that the way we are living our lives is eroding our capacity for deep, sustained, perceptive attention. One study also showed that the mere presence of a mobile phone reduces our cognitive capacity *significantly*, even when switched off.

The implication is that technology breaks can make the difference to improving our physical and emotional wellbeing. But for the love of Steve Jobs, don't go cold turkey! Try an hour phone-free, then increase it slowly. Make sure if you are with a partner or friend they do the same.

Tips for technology breaks

Choose to unplug from your social media during the day — at mealtimes, when going into a meeting, when focusing on an important task or having a face-to-face conversation.

When faced with a time gap during your day, make the conscious decision not to fill it by updating your Twitter feed or sending another text. Pause and look around you. Observe other people: notice their interactions, their expression, their activities; re-engage with what's going on around you.

Take time to reflect on your social interactions at the end of the day. What went well? How did you deal with a difficult conversation, or a colleague who was upset?

Why monotasking is the new black

Multitasking, the myth beloved of parents everywhere that we can focus our attention on more than one task at a time, is a physiological impossibility, unless you happen to be in the 1 to 2 per cent (according to research by Watson and Strayer) of the population who are supertaskers and use a different part of their brain to divide attention. Until we have learned how we can do this for ourselves, the advice remains the same.

We are not Superman or Wonder Woman, and even if we put our underpants on over our clothes, we cannot fly. Not even in an invisible jet.

WE CANNOT MULTITASK. NOT IF WE ARE FEMALE, NOT IF WE ARE YOUNG. NOT. AT. ALL.

As figure 5.3 shows, the problem with multitasking is that we are asking our brain to do something it wasn't designed for.

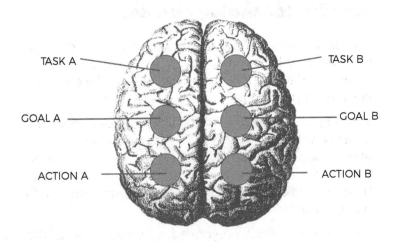

SPLITTING TASKS COSTS TIME, ENERGY AND ACCURACY

Figure 5.3: the myth of multitasking

We use our prefrontal cortex to focus attention. It is an extremely energy-hungry part of the brain and a confined space. While the received wisdom has been that we can hold up to seven (plus or minus two) items in the front of mind at any one time, this has been shown to be the case only for simple digits. More complex items take up more thinking room, meaning we can probably hold onto only one or two ideas at any one time. Increasing focus to give an item our full attention limits the space to one.

When we attempt to multitask, our obliging brain helps by splitting the two items and allocating one to each hemisphere. Don't even think of going for three, because if you remember the definition of *hemi*, there's a 'half' in it, and this isn't a lesson in non-Euclidean geometry.

Our hemispheres take the two items and alternate our attention between them extremely quickly. This gives us the magical illusion that we are multitasking, when in fact we are just giving half our attention to each task, and probably messing each of them up quite effectively and thoroughly. In fact, studies by Rubinstein and others have revealed 'multitasking' can reduce performance and productivity by 40 per cent.

It is cognitively exhausting, reduces memory and is associated with an increased amount of error.

Strategies for focus

Want to be a high-performance thinker? Here's the secret: monotasking.

This is a bit complex, so I'll try to make it as user-friendly as possible. It's sometimes hard to take the jargon out of medical explanations, I admit, but here goes.

DO ONE THING AT A TIME, GIVE IT YOUR FULL AND UNDIVIDED ATTENTION, AND DO IT WELL.

Well, that went better than I thought it would.

Regaining our attention and managing distractions is possible because we can exercise our attention just like a muscle. The more we practise, the better we get and sometimes just a few simple changes in our work practices can make a big difference.

Working smarter begins with choosing where to place your focus and creating the environment that best suits your attention-on brain. Here are 10 leads on how best to create that environment.

» *Pick a quiet place to allow your brain to think in a less stressed state.* Studies by Evans and Johnson have shown that noise is a stress and distraction that diminishes our ability to focus. Many people will tell you they can only work while listening to music. They have trained their brain to tolerate the sound, but the brain is still stressed and does not habituate to noise. If you must have sound, make it music that you like but are not actively engaged with. Why? Because, paradoxically, music or other noise can be used as a focusing tool to block out other distractors. That's why some people can work well in coffee shops: they have become acclimatised to the cacophony of extraneous noise to the extent they no longer consciously hear it (though the subconscious does).

» *Practise your focus,* just as you would during a music lesson. Set aside 10 minutes to pay close attention to a task you do regularly. It could be reading, listening to music or preparing a meal. As you do the task consciously, think about what you are doing, and then test yourself on something you have learned.

» *Prioritise the following day's work.* By sorting out the next day's top priorities before the end of your day, your mind is already focusing on the things to be done, even before you have arrived and started working on them.

» *Fight for three.* Peter Cook, thought leader and author of *The New Rules of Management,* shares the wise advice that you fight to get your top three priorities done every day. Having identified what they are, choose to focus and work only on these until they are completed. This builds on Bob Pozen's suggestion that we allocate 70 to 80 per cent of our working day to our top three priorities.

» *Manage your inbox.* Bob Pozen's advice is to respond immediately to email that merits it and junk the rest. He firmly believes in the OHIO principle: 'Only Handle It Once'.

» *Schedule meetings for B- or C-class thinking time.* Our best thinking times are brief. In other words, we have to treat our thinking time as an investment in quality, like really good wine or, with apologies to vegetarian readers, like the best quality Wagyu beef. You want to enjoy it at its best. Those lesser cuts of sirloin, gravy beef and mince correspond to the other times when perhaps we don't require quality thinking time. If you do your best creative work in the morning, schedule appointments and meetings for the afternoon. As a rule, your best thinking time in any 24-hour period is most likely to be in the morning, usually the first three to four hours after getting up. That's why developing the habit of getting a few items done quickly BEFORE you start your working day is a brilliant way to prime yourself for continuing great performance.

» *Unplug regularly.* As already mentioned, this means taking regular brain breaks, the pit stops necessary to fuel up for another lap of grand prix business performance. Don't neglect regular technology breaks either. In a study by Gloria Mark (from the University of California) and others in which office workers were denied access to their computers and smartphones for five days, it was found that while they complained bitterly at first, they then showed increased productivity. What's more, individual blood-pressure readings went down and they subjectively reported feeling better and less stressed.

» *Play some video games.* Yes, video games, especially those fast, action-packed games (not necessarily Grand Theft Auto 5), are great for building attention. Daphne Bavalier, a neuroscientist, has shown how video games make our brain smarter, better, faster and stronger. The average gamer is in their thirties, so these games are clearly not just for the kids. While it is recognised that overplaying certain video games can lead to problems with addictive behaviour, for the vast majority, playing games for an hour or so several nights a week has a number of positives.

Gamers develop sharper visual acuity, which can help them pick out a stranger in a crowd and observe small details. They are also better at tracking more objects simultaneously. Games boost our attentional networks (alerting, orienting and executive), driving — you guessed it — plasticity. Gamers are also better at task switching with less cognitive cost compared with non-gamers.

Training on action games can help people improve their performance in difficult mental tasks, and this improvement persists for months after the training has finished.

» *Take regular holidays.* Take a real vacation, without your laptop, computer tablet or smartphone, and rediscover the joys of conversation, of seeing the beauty of the world around you, and fully engage all your senses in your experience.

» *Avoid 'multitasking', or mythitasking.* Yes, we know this is a no-brainer yet we all try to do it. Why? Because we think we can — we may even think we're good at it — and we believe it saves us time and energy. It's such a pity this is wrong at all levels.

KEY 6
Mindset
Does your attitude suck?

Think of a chessboard and the pieces on it. The knights, riding out to face the battle without fear or favour. The bishops, determining the direction of the strategy with their unexpected diagonal movements. The king? A mere figurehead, but we won't tell him if you don't, because naturally it's the queen who is truly the bee all (pardon the pun) and end all of the board. Then there are the pawns. Are they cannon fodder, sulkily accepting their lot, or are they simply waiting to take on their next role as a knight in game two?

As in a game of chess, the ability to succeed as an organisation, irrespective of sector or industry, depends less on the talent pool than on the state of mind of all the players. Pawn or prince, attitude will determine performance in all employment levels of a corporation or business.

> ### Brainy facts about your attitude and the way it affects you at work
>
> » Attitude is always a choice. You can change it. If you are struggling with a problem, don't give up
>
> *(continued)*

Brainy facts about your attitude and the way it affects you at work *(cont'd)*

in despair and say 'it's/I'm useless'. You simply haven't found one of the possible solutions yet.

» Our attitude or mindset is orientated in one of two ways: fixed (closed) or growth (open).

» A fixed mindset takes the stance that talent is innate; you are born intelligent or you're not. A growth mindset will recognise that there is always opportunity to learn, stretch and improve (see figure 6.1).

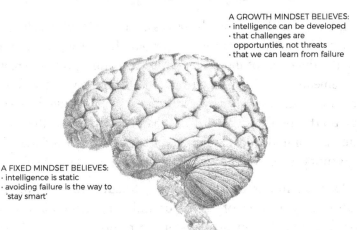

A GROWTH MINDSET BELIEVES:
· intelligence can be developed
· that challenges are opportunities, not threats
· that we can learn from failure

A FIXED MINDSET BELIEVES:
· intelligence is static
· avoiding failure is the way to 'stay smart'

Figure 6.1: fixed vs growth mindset

» A skilled negotiator uses a growth mindset to explore alternatives and consider all options.

» A leader uses a growth mindset to nurture and develop potential talent in their team or company.

» An entrepreneur uses a growth mindset to embrace change and possibility thinking to lead to transformation.

What's with the attitude?

I often get asked why attitude matters. My usual response is, 'Have you ever worked [or lived] with someone who has an "attitude"? How did that make you *feel* generally? And, most importantly, how did it impact your ability to *focus* on your work?'

In her book *Mindset: The New Psychology of Success*, Carol Dweck describes mindset as the single quality that separates those who succeed the most from those who don't. This is why our attitude matters. It has nothing to do with intelligence. Have you ever attended a school reunion and discovered that it wasn't necessarily the 'clever' kids who had achieved the most or enjoyed the greatest commercial or personal kudos?

Success has far more to do with 'fluid' intelligence, tenacity and belief.

Our attitude or mindset is not something we are born with. It evolves gradually, refined by our experiences and who we spend our time with. Naturally, our earliest attitude formation is highly influenced by our parents or caregivers, how they interact with us and others, their values, beliefs and behaviours.

THE ATTITUDE WE FORM IN CHILDHOOD WILL STICK WITH US – AND IF IT'S LESS THAN STELLAR, WE HAVE TO MAKE A CONSCIOUS CHOICE TO CHANGE IT.

Dweck's research reveals how our use of language when praising our kids can have a profound impact on attitudinal development. Subtle differences in intonation, wording and phrasing can lead a child at age two to form a belief about how good they are likely to be at maths when starting school at age seven. This, in turn, will impact on future career choices and can lead to a gap in gender equity within certain industries and sectors.

For example; boys are more likely to be praised for their effort: 'Well done for trying so hard!' Girls are praised for ability: 'Good girl, you are so clever!'

The problem is that praising for intelligence can set a child up for limiting self-beliefs that they carry across childhood and into adult life. Being praised for being clever induces a short-lasting feeling of pride, which leads to the thinking that intelligence is what matters. Therefore, to be respected or successful, you must always show you are smart. This can then lead to situations where a child with a reputation for being 'smart' becomes risk-averse, as they don't want to be revealed as being dumb or stupid.

Conversely, being told by a teacher or parent that 'you'll never amount to anything!' can either motivate the growth mindset of 'I'll show you, you are so wrong!' or the fixed mindset of 'I'm thick, I can't do maths, it's not for me'.

MINDSET MATTERS BECAUSE IT PREDETERMINES WHICH PATHS WE CHOOSE AND OUR EVENTUAL OUTCOME.

MINDSET OVER MATTER

The modern workplace requires leaders and their teams to manipulate the information they hold in a way that will prove most useful to them and to their stakeholders. The world is a furious and uncertain place. Business must, if not constantly boom, then at least grow and prosper over time. If you can't see how or where to use certain data or ideas to make this happen, or you feel threatened by others who do get the big picture, you will quickly be left behind.

Since 2010, Dweck and others have been conducting research into whether companies as a whole held a *growth* or *fixed* mindset, and the impact this had on their employees. Based on staff statements from seven Fortune 1000 companies, they found that each company appeared to have a consensus around mindset, and it affected the way their employees performed:

> ... employees at companies with a fixed mindset often said that just a small handful of 'star' workers were highly valued. The employees who reported this were less committed than employees at growth-mindset companies and didn't think the company had their back. They worried about failing and so pursued fewer innovative projects. They regularly kept secrets, cut corners, and cheated to try to get ahead.

Conversely, those in growth-minded companies saw the world somewhat differently:

» 47 per cent were more likely to state their colleagues are trustworthy

» 34 per cent were more likely to feel a strong sense of ownership and commitment to their company

» 65 per cent were more likely to say the company supports risk taking

» 49 per cent were more likely to say the company fosters innovation.

It appears that an organisation with a growth mindset holds a powerful tool for building allegiance, loyalty, trust and business growth.

The million-dollar question that will reveal a great deal about your own current attitude is this:

WHICH MINDSET STYLE WOULD YOU CURRENTLY PREFER TO BE WORKING WITH?

I'M OPEN-MINDED, BUT...

How open-minded are you? We like to think we are very liberal in our thought processes and theoretical views, but unfortunately our thinking doesn't always match these beliefs. Humans are complex, with levels of internal biases, both conscious and subconscious, that strongly influence how we react or respond in a given situation.

For example, you hear on the news that the managing director of a large company has just stepped down following allegations of fraud. Be honest with yourself. Is your response along the lines of, 'That rat! How did a [lots of rude words] like him get to be in such a position of authority and control? He deserves to go to jail for a very long time'.

Or do you think, 'Well, fair shake of the sauce bottle, he's probably going to the big house. Still, you never know. Innocent till proved guilty after all! At least he's done the right thing and stepped aside while the allegations are dealt with'.

I think you know what I am going to tell you, apart from 'that's some pretty spectacular vernacular'. If you are closed-minded, your perspective will be the black and white: 'It's open and shut — send him down, your Honour'. An open mindset will give the benefit of the doubt until all the facts are in.

WORKPLACE PERSPECTIVE

We've all heard of the saying 'people who live in glass houses ...', so let's translate that to the smeared perspex of the workplace cubicle. Mindset in business is a massive part of our own success story — and can impact hugely on that of others.

» How do you view the young man with the impressive CV who turns up to an interview dressed in jeans and a T-shirt, compared with the other young interviewee who has a less impressive CV but is smartly turned out in a new suit?

» What about that annoying person in a meeting who clearly likes the sound of their own voice and constantly drowns out any other viewpoint? How are you going to react when your boss advises you they are to be your project buddy for the next three months?

Keeping an open mind helps us to look at the bigger picture, rather than being bogged down in the minutiae and the drama. It also means we may actually notice the value in someone whom we don't necessarily find personally appealing, but who has work skills that are useful to the organisation and to us as leaders. This is about using our mindset to future-proof our own success stories — and that means being brainy in terms of attitude.

NOTICING THOSE TIMES WHEN YOUR THINKING MAY BE LIMITED BY YOUR OWN BELIEFS PROVIDES THE OPPORTUNITY FOR SELF-DIRECTED CHANGE.

Having the capacity as a manager or leader to keep an open mind to all possibilities is vital to ensure that the best decision is made in a given set of circumstances.

It can be hard to admit to, let alone challenge, our own limiting beliefs, but what about dealing with others who operate from a fixed mindset?

'It won't work.'

'It's hopeless.'

'Already tried that, mate.'

'I can't be bothered.'

'Who cares?'

Exposure to new ideas, new concepts and new people can be threatening to our brain and the status quo. Giving ourselves permission to try something new, simply changing our perspective, opens us up to a world of possibility. What this means is that when things go wrong — and let's face it, they often do — it's our choice of response that matters.

As Maya Angelou said, 'You may not control all the events that happen to you but you can decide not to be reduced by them'.

High-performance thinking means developing the skillset required to manage our lives well, not just when life is sunny and bright, but also in tougher times when difficult decisions have to be made or endured.

The power of belief

'Whether you think you can, or think you can't, you're right.'
Henry Ford

The self-fulfilling prophecy is alive and kicking. The strength of our beliefs really does make a difference to how well we perform, whether in an exam or in our work.

Our personal success is also fuelled by the beliefs of those around us. In the media it's not uncommon to hear comments from a coach or sports commentator about the next 'rising star'. But how much impact does this external belief system really have?

As it turns out, a lot.

This was shown in a study carried out back in the 1960s by Rosenthal and Jacobson. Teachers at an elementary school were advised that some of their students had been determined through IQ tests to be 'spurters' and would perform better than their classmates over the course of the year. This was untrue; there was no such difference between the kids. But the results showed that those students whose teachers now had higher expectations for their performance did indeed get better academic results.

The implication here is that how your boss views you, and how you *believe* your boss views you, will influence your performance. It shouldn't come as a shock to learn that if you feel nurtured, supported and believed in, your confidence is higher and your performance rises. Similarly, a leader who sees their own behaviour being rewarded by employee participation will engage in those behaviours that perpetuate mutual trust and respect.

Leadership programs depend on this. Identifying those seen as having leadership potential will elevate those individuals' career prospects much more quickly than if they are not recognised in this way.

There is a caveat here, and it goes back to the 'you're such a smart girl' scenario. Rewarding intelligence rather than effort will inhibit us from developing our true potential. Why?

> **BECAUSE IF WE HAVE A FIXED MINDSET AND ARE GIVEN A CHALLENGE BEYOND WHAT *WE BELIEVE* WE ARE CAPABLE OF, WE SIMPLY WON'T DELIVER ON ANYTHING MORE THAN OUR 'THIS IS WHAT I CAN DO – NO MORE, NO LESS'.**

This not infrequently shows up where a candidate is selected for a particular role based on previous performance and experience. The employer's expectation is that their new employee, whose CV reads so well, will step up to the challenge and perform beyond expectations. But if the candidate is fearful they will be shown up for getting something wrong, they will often underperform.

This is incredibly frustrating both for them and of course for their employer who had such high hopes. It can be a particular problem for a closed-mindset employee who fails to recognise they are underperforming and sees only that they are working to the tasks set.

Irrational rationalisation

Geoff is a clever guy. He was dux at school, works hard in his job and looks after his health and family. But over the years he has continued to miss out on promotions and on enjoying the success others thought would come his way.

The problem? His fixed mindset and lack of self-belief.

He sees others doing better and attributes their success to luck or knowing the right people. When yet another opportunity passed him by, he justified it by claiming, 'I wasn't ready', 'The other candidate was much more confident' or 'I didn't think the position was a good fit anyway'.

Using negative self-talk disguised as rationalisation diminishes our ability to keep things in perspective and to question the validity of our beliefs.

If Geoff checked in with his thoughts, he might realise they have little basis in fact.

Have you met a Geoff, someone who appears to have so much talent and potential, yet never realises their promise?

A fixed mindset and lack of self-belief can miss so much.

One of the more quirky research findings on the difference between a fixed and a growth mindset is that when we are praised more for our intelligence we are three times more likely to lie about our performance!

Being praised too highly for mental performance not only reduces future performance, it increases cheating and makes people less adaptive to proposed change in the work environment. Perhaps we should be less surprised when academic fraud is discovered. In the academic world intelligence remains very highly valued.

The benefits of a growth mindset have been shown to include:

» better academic and sporting performance

» higher levels of motivation to tackle more difficult tasks

» greater satisfaction from 'having a go'

» more rewarding relationships

» even being a better parent.

For the individual: becoming brain type 'be positive'

The first thing is to determine if you are operating with a growth or fixed mindset. This will involve tuning in to your internal dialogue when faced with a problem or challenge.

Check in first at hotel reality

Listen to your thoughts or voice when you respond to a challenge. Be aware also that you may think differently in different circumstances and on different days, depending on how tired or stressed you are.

Maybe you've had a bad start to your day. Maybe you overslept, or you forgot to bring to work the important file you spent several hours working on the previous night. Your boss is grouchy, and in your rush to sort things out you knock your coffee cup over your laptop.

If you have a fixed mindset, your internal dialogue may begin with a few choice expletives, blaming others — your boss, the traffic that added to your lateness and caused the spilt coffee. You may be telling yourself it's always like this when you are under the pump. You berate yourself for your stupidity in forgetting that file.

With a growth mindset, you may be grateful that spilling that coffee didn't damage your laptop. You know you can easily nip home to grab the file. You understand your boss is grouchy because he is under pressure to deliver the monthly targets and because he is worried about his elderly mother, who recently had a stroke and is unlikely to be able to return to her home after she leaves hospital.

Know your choices

Remember, you don't have to buy into the negative. If you really want to wallow in self-pity or anger when things haven't gone your way, that's okay, so long as you are aware that you can 'flip' to look at things differently when you choose to. You may find exercising on a treadmill boring and hard work. But what if instead of dreading the time you will spend on it, you look at the benefit that being fitter will bring to your life?

So often it is not so much the challenges we face that are the issue, but how we choose to respond to them. I am certain you know of people who have faced adversity and survived, and even come through with a smile on their face and full of gratitude.

As a medical practitioner, I have spent a lot of time over the years helping people come to terms with a difficult diagnosis, and the disappointment and fear it triggers. What has been very apparent is the enormous role attitude plays in determining an outcome. It is humbling to see how a young mother facing imminent death prepares her family to cope and continue to live after she dies. Witnessing how a person comes to terms with loss of a limb or disfigurement can help us to keep our own difficulties in perspective. Seeing a person living with a positive attitude makes it a lot easier to choose a more optimistic outlook for ourselves.

Watch your language

If you hear yourself saying, 'I just can't do that', change it to, 'I'll give it a go', or, 'Last time I made a complete dog's breakfast of it, but I've been practising and I think I've cracked the code'. Instead of telling yourself you are a failure for not getting the promotion you wanted, think, 'I wasn't the person they were looking for today, but I'll get a chance another time'.

This is not about false hope or fake optimism, but about keeping things in perspective. Change your language to reflect your ability to turn things around.

Possibility thinking gives you the prospect of a different outcome another time. You haven't got there yet, but with continued perseverance you may. One of the key attributes needed to cope with ongoing change is giving yourself permission to not always succeed right away. As our world gets busier and faster, giving yourself permission to keep on trying makes it easier to adjust.

Having a massively plastic brain means you can continue to learn new things, process new information, acquire new skills and embed new habits across your lifespan.

Keep practising!

Look for opportunities to stretch your capabilities. Focus on continually learning and getting better. Reflect on what didn't work and what you could do differently next time. Remember, it's the effort you put in that pays the dividends and makes you feel good about your achievements.

For the organisation: keeping the door ajar

Good leaders and managers adopt an open-door policy and are seen to be accessible to staff.

Develop a framework for positive and honest feedback

Hearing out complaints and grievances without judgement or ridicule boosts open conversations. Enquiring how the employee would address the issue invites dialogue.

» 'How can we help you to do better?'

» 'What is it you are looking for in the next step of your career?'

» 'How can we support you?'

Accepting failure as a lesson to learn from, and aiming to do better as a result next time, rather than as a red stamp 'fail', encourages staff to look for better solutions or alternatives.

Praising effort by staff, regardless of outcome, matters

Coming second (not losing, coming second — re-language it!) in a grand final is never a good feeling, but the coach or manager who rewards the team effort for what was achieved throughout the season will inspire the team to greater success next year.

Ask what your staff finds exciting or motivating about their work

And look for opportunities to encourage that enthusiasm. Look to provide employees with a bit of a stretch that they can aspire to, and reward their efforts.

Avoid micromanagement

Give individuals the chance to show for themselves what they are capable of.

Build brain awareness about mindset in the organisation

Teaching people how they can empower themselves through understanding how the human brain works, works!

KEY 7
Healthy stress
Creating a brain-safe environment

Think of the last time you played sport, or even were involved in an intense game of trivia down at the pub. Your heart is beating faster, your blood pressure is higher. You *really* need to win — even if you won't admit it to yourself (especially when it comes to the trivia). Game over, you come home victorious. Don't you feel great? You have been flying by the seat of your pants, making quick decisions, razor-sharp thinking ...

And yet you have also been quite stressed.

The brain's primary function is to keep us safe. If danger looms we react fast. When we feel safe, we have the luxury of taking the slower thinking route involving the prefrontal cortex to consider our response.

Acting on reflex denies us the time required to consider all options and make the best decisions. As a result, we tend to believe it's our emotions that determine how we react at any given moment. The reality is in fact the opposite: we rely on our emotional regulation to ensure we respond appropriately.

Brainy facts about emotions, stress and work

Emotion is vital to decision making, our ability to learn and remember, distinguishing individual differences, and determining our resilience and adaptability to challenges in our environment.

So in the workplace emotional regulation is highly desirable:

» to enable compliance on health and safety issues

» for effective communication, keeping conversations as dialogue

» to allow for diversity of thought

» for better learning and memory

» to promote collaboration, engagement, trust and relatedness

» for emotional wellbeing.

The problem is that in many workplaces today showing emotion or 'being emotional' is often seen in a negative light. With reports of increasing levels of stress, burnout, and mental health issues including anxiety, depression and unhappiness in the workplace, clearly emotional wellbeing is not being adequately dealt with. Bullying, discrimination, lack of trust and lack of autonomy provide the perfect cocktail for a toxic workplace.

Those companies that dismiss the relevance of emotion to their business are in denial over the fundamentally human desire to feel safe, included and valued.

Ask someone about stress and they will usually tell you it's a bad thing. It's bad for your brain and your body and can make you sick. Which is true, *if* the stress you are experiencing is chronic, severe and overwhelming your normal coping mechanisms. Yet stress is a completely normal part of our everyday lives. If we didn't have *any* stress, we wouldn't have the impetus to get out of bed in the morning, let alone get on and do anything.

Stress is a physiological response to a change in our environment and is designed primarily to keep us safe. Being able to distinguish between danger and safety is obviously very important to our survival. It's like being able to tell the difference between hot and cold or sharp and smooth to the touch.

Eustress is the term given to the everyday stress that keeps us going, that allows us to look forward to the challenges we face each day, the excitement of a new job, a new project at work or a new relationship. It's those butterflies in your stomach as you prepare to deliver your first presentation, shoot your first goal or meet your partner's parents.

What we perceive to be stressful (that is, outside our comfort level) varies from person to person, event to event and moment to moment. Jo finds it stressful talking to people she doesn't know at networking events, whereas John stresses over being even one minute late for an appointment.

Stress leave

You may find a work situation so stressful it leaves you feeling chronically fatigued to the point of exhaustion. If you see no possibility of being able to take some time off to relax and recharge, then you run the risk that your immune system will be impaired to the point of not being able to fight off minor but inconvenient illnesses such as colds and 'flu. Your risk of developing more serious conditions, such as heart disease, mental illness or even cancer, also increase.

CAREGIVERS ARE KNOWN TO BE AT INCREASED RISK OF STRESS-RELATED ILLNESS; CHRONIC SEVERE STRESS IS ASSOCIATED WITH EXCESSIVE RELEASE OF CORTISOL, ONE OF THE STRESS HORMONES PRODUCED BY THE ADRENAL MEDULLA.

But there is something else at play here. And it comes down to belief.

Kelly McGonigal, a psychologist at Stanford University, believes we need to make stress our friend and stop making it Public Enemy Number One. In her TED talk she shares the idea that we can produce a different outcome by reprogramming our belief as to whether the stress we are under makes us sick. She looked at the evidence that challenged the long-held belief that being exposed to severe chronic stress inevitably makes us sick.

In one study, 30000 adult Americans were tracked over a period of eight years. They were initially asked to record how much stress they had experienced over the previous 12 months and whether they believed this was potentially harmful to their health. The researchers followed up by checking on death records.

That might sound a bit morbid, but the results were interesting. The study confirmed that having more stress in your life is associated with a higher level of morbidity. No unexpected news there. Those who reported being under significant stress over that time interval had a 43 per cent higher risk of dying compared with those who didn't report being overstressed.

Remarkably, however, this increased death rate showed up only in those who expressed the belief that stress was harmful to health. Those who didn't share that belief, despite experiencing high levels of stress, had a lower risk of dying compared with the group who reported having less stress.

IT'S NOT THE AMOUNT OR SEVERITY OF THE STRESS THAT HARMS US: IT IS OUR BELIEF IN WHETHER OR NOT WE WILL SUSTAIN HARM FROM THE STRESS.

When we feel severely stressed, the physiological changes we notice in our body may include a pounding heart, trembling knees, sweaty palms, nausea and that horrible stomach churn. These unpleasant symptoms act as a warning to our conscious awareness that this is a place of danger and perhaps we should skedaddle to safety, quick smart (see figure 7.1).

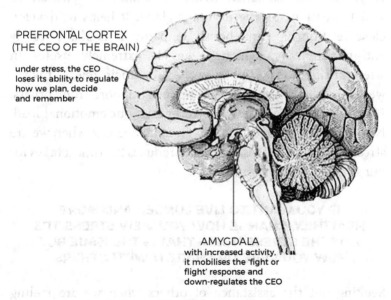

PREFRONTAL CORTEX
(THE CEO OF THE BRAIN)

under stress, the CEO loses its ability to regulate how we plan, decide and remember

AMYGDALA
with increased activity, it mobilises the 'fight or flight' response and down-regulates the CEO

Figure 7.1: the fight-or-flight response

But what if we changed our perspective about this?

For those affected by anxiety and panic disorders, the physiological symptoms we recognise trigger a rapid spiral down into thoughts of fear and dread. Changing our thinking from 'Oh no, here we go again' to 'Great, this is a good sign! My body is energised to meet this new challenge' keeps the thinking part of our brain engaged and minimises the stress response.

When the body is under stress, the arterial pressure normally increases, leading to an increase in blood pressure. This is fine in a short-term stressful situation. Chronic stress, however, can potentially lead to the development of hypertension and heart disease.

Why caring is sharing

Oxytocin, the so-called 'trust hormone', is released in social situations by the pituitary gland. It helps us develop close relationships and boosts empathy. It is also potently anti-inflammatory, which makes it extremely useful in stressful situations. Higher levels of oxytocin released when we are under stress drive us to seek support from others. Human connection allows us to lighten our emotional load. Not only this, the act of caring for someone else when we are stressed helps create resilience and reduces the time it takes for our stress levels to normalise.

IF YOU WANT TO LIVE LONGER AND MORE HEALTHILY, CHANGE HOW YOU VIEW STRESS. IT'S NOT THE STRESS ITSELF THAT IS THE ISSUE BUT HOW YOU VIEW OR SHARE IT WITH OTHERS.

Seeking out the assistance of others when we are feeling burdened by severe chronic stress is extremely important to our wellbeing. It might even help us live longer.

How we choose to reduce our emotional load of difficult circumstances will vary according to what the problem is and how much it is interfering with our ability to stay on task and feel well. Perhaps you've noticed too that we seek solace from our emotional pain by engaging in activities we would avoid at other times.

We rationalise why we do this through what is called cognitive dissonance. You may have given up smoking for your health six months ago, but today you justify lighting up because you've had a really bad day and you know it will help you relax.

Our perception of the 'right' way to make ourselves feel better sometimes may be quite 'wrong' for us at other times. But does this matter? It is our belief at the time that counts. If we believe drinking or smoking will make us feel better we do it, even though we know that relying on this type of crutch is not helpful in the longer term.

Workplace stress is not going to disappear. What matters is having the right set of strategies to help us navigate the ups and downs of everyday life and work so we feel in control (even if it's only partial control) of our circumstances and emotions and can stay in balance.

Managing stress

Reviewing the issue of workplace stress adequately would require another book! However, stress management and emotional regulation in the workplace has to be a given. Every person at work, from the CEO down, needs the right tools to minimise bad stress in order to function at a higher level and enjoy a greater level of happiness and wellbeing.

Which method you use to manage stress doesn't matter. What does matter is being aware that your stress levels may be too high and that you need to do something about it.

IDENTIFY THE CULPRIT OR CULPRITS

With so many things going on in our lives, our stress usually has not just one source but a complicity of causes, like the many layers of a mille-feuille cake.

IDENTIFY WHAT YOU CAN CHANGE AND WHAT YOU CAN'T

The first rule of stress management is to worry about things that are under your control, not things that aren't. Stressing about issues you cannot change is simply a waste of time and energy, both of which could be diverted to more productive and enjoyable activities. Let go. Easy to say, of course, but unless you choose to change here, nothing else will change.

CHOOSE YOUR STRESS REDUCTION PLAN

This might include any of a variety of different methods. There's no one-size-fits-all here. Different events might see you using different methods. And that doesn't matter so long as, whatever method you use, you feel you are making progress and feeling better for it.

IMPLEMENT YOUR STRESS REDUCTION PLAN

Practising a relaxation technique daily helps to build resilience and coping skills. It doesn't have to take long or be very complicated. It might involve:

» aerobic exercise or dancing

» socialising with family and friends

» switching off from technology regularly

» taking holidays when they are due and planning long weekend breaks in between

» taking up a new hobby or interest outside work, such as painting, gardening or cooking

» learning yoga, tai chi, meditation or Pilates

» playing or listening to music.

Psychological techniques to alleviate stress

A number of psychological practices can also help to alleviate stress, perhaps the most significant being *labelling* and *reframing*.

LABELLING

Putting our feelings into words helps to dissipate some of the emotional intensity we experience. Acknowledging that you feel angry or sad and saying it out loud decreases activity in the amygdala and increases it in our executive prefrontal cortex. In others words, hearing ourselves verbalise what we are feeling makes it easier for our conscious mind to rein in the over-exuberance of the emotional amygdala. The effect can be similar to what we experience when we talk things through with a friend or jot thoughts down in a journal.

Sometimes the simplest of techniques can make the biggest difference in maintaining our mental health and wellbeing.

REFRAMING

James Gross, a leader in emotional regulation, has commented that 'reframing should be in the water we drink'. What he means is that teaching people how to cognitively reappraise a situation can save an enormous amount of unnecessary angst. He likens it to a cost-free cognitive emotional neutraliser. We feel better simply by deliberately choosing to reinterpret a given situation.

Suppression has been shown to be the worst form of emotional regulation, because rather than diminishing an emotional response it heightens the amygdala response. Worse still, it has been shown to reduce memory in the person actively trying to suppress how they feel and to increase blood pressure in others around them. Rather than having one upset person, you can end up with a crowd!

In the past, the Brits have had a bit of a reputation for emotional suppression. It was seen as a sign of weakness to show how you felt. Heaving bosoms and repressed expressions of emotion were all the rage in the Brontë era, but they clearly were not a very emotionally balanced lot.

Reframing can help us move away from negative appraisal of a situation for which there is no basis other than our bad mood.

You are already feeling frazzled because you have an important deadline looming, you've skipped lunch because you felt compelled to keep working, and when you scoot out to your local coffee shop for a much-needed java pick-me-up you witness a young mother seemingly ignoring the high jinks of her three young children, who are cavorting loudly and somewhat dangerously between the café tables.

Do you mutter under your breath about 'some parents' who seem to have 'no control over their kids'? Do you complain loudly to the girl at the counter that this behaviour needs to be dealt with — now? Or do you ask the young mum if there is anything you can do to help as it seems her kids are a bit of a handful?

BEING TOLD YOU HAVE A 90 PER CENT CHANCE OF SURVIVING AN OPERATION SOUNDS A LOT BETTER THAN BEING TOLD YOU HAVE A 10 PER CENT CHANCE OF DYING, YET THE ODDS ARE THE SAME.

The frame of reference we give to a situation determines our emotional response, and the filter we apply leads to our creating a new emotional state.

Reframing needs practice. As with other brain activities, the more we use it the more accomplished we become. For example, when chewing over a difficult problem or relationship issue, it can help to write down or mentally construct a list of different perspectives to consider.

As the law frequently reminds us, there are usually at least two sides to every story. Considering all the evidence impartially helps us to identify which is the correct path for us to follow.

Building organisational resilience can include:

» encouraging open dialogue to consider all viewpoints

» asking staff to come forward with suggestions to resolve a challenge they face, rather than simply asking for help

» creating a work culture of tolerance and acceptance of diversity.

Mobilising the brain to learn

W. Edwards Deming reminds us, 'Learning is not compulsory, but neither is survival'. Learning remains a critically important competency in organisations, yet formal organisational learning or training currently accounts for only 10 to 20 per cent of workplace learning; 80 per cent takes place informally 'on the job', thus lacking design or strategy.

To mobilise our brains to learn efficiently we first need to recognise the changed nature and speed of the working environment. Technology and access to data have become so pervasive that we are now 'online' 24/7, hyper-stimulated with multiple communication channels vying for our attention. We have adapted by reducing our attention time to different tasks. This is why when web surfing we will spend an average of four seconds on a web page before clicking to the next. It's why we skim-read articles just looking for the salient points, perhaps reading only the first 100 or 150 words before moving on. We have also reduced the length of the messages we exchange, as exemplified by Twitter's 140-character limit.

Increasing demands on our time and the complexity of our work mean allocating time and energy to learning modules is becoming increasingly difficult. Organisations are reluctant to allow staff to spend too long away from their desks. They also want the reassurance that there will be a return on their investment of the time and money required. The result is that businesses and staff are looking for shorter chunks of focused learning rather than full training days.

The problem is that our fragmented and shortened attention spans have led to a reduction of the depth of understanding of our learning.

Learning changes the brain and shapes who we are. It determines how we respond, cope and adapt to change and opportunity. Different generations learn differently because they are wired differently.

SAFETY FIRST

Of all the millions of bytes of information that the brain receives every second, only 2000 or so make it through the first filter, the reticular activating system. The second filter, the amygdala, helps determine where we direct the incoming information — either to the prefrontal cortex or to the subconscious. The prefrontal cortex and amygdala join in a delicate dance, each vying to take the lead (see figure 7.2).

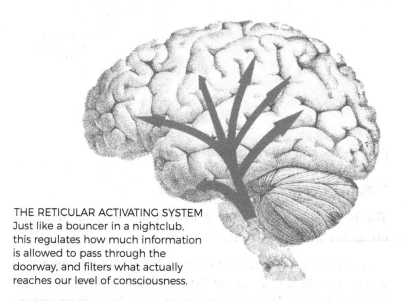

THE RETICULAR ACTIVATING SYSTEM
Just like a bouncer in a nightclub,
this regulates how much information
is allowed to pass through the
doorway, and filters what actually
reaches our level of consciousness.

Figure 7.2: filtering information

If we sense danger, the amygdala, being stronger and faster, takes over, denying access to the prefrontal cortex, which is why we find it harder to take things in when we are stressed.

A staff member who is experiencing a lot of stress either at home or in the workplace is not going to be with you mentally. Their amygdala will be on high alert, and even though they may be sitting there, eyes open, apparently listening, they may be taking in little of the information being presented.

Evian Gordon, a neuroscientist, proposed that the brain operates either in a 'towards state where it anticipates reward' or an 'away state where it wants you to get the heck outta there immediately' (see figure 7.3, overleaf).

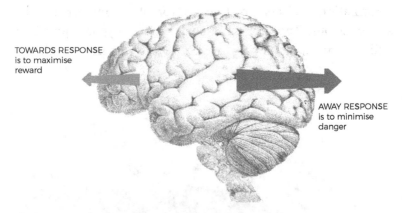

Figure 7.3: the away–towards model

TOWARDS MENTAL STRETCH

The best place of learning is a brain-safe environment that promotes the *towards state*.

This is about checking in prior to the training to ascertain where people are at an individual level, connecting with previous knowledge and experience, and then incorporating some fun and humour to help keep everyone relaxed. It's also about providing a mental stretch. If the information is presented in a boring way (think death by PowerPoint) or covers material you are already familiar with, you are likely to quickly switch off and perhaps seek refuge under the cover of checking your Twitter feed or Facebook updates.

Peter Drucker, the founder of modern management, summed up the need for organisational learning nicely when he said, 'We now accept the fact that learning is a lifelong process of keeping abreast of change. And the most pressing task is to teach people how to learn'. Which is true, as is the need to recognise that a one-size-fits-all approach to learning won't work in a workplace that comprises five different generations.

Technology is contributing increasingly to workplace learning. It is interactive fun and can be designed to allow participants to travel at their own pace, with logon progress that can be monitored by both the individual and the person operating the program. Video games in particular are often structured to reflect your current level of activity and then provide what neurologist and educator Dr Judy Willis calls 'an achievable challenge'. If you have ever played video games you will recognise the thrill of passing each level and feeling inherently rewarded. That extra dose of dopamine makes us feel good.

Video games have a bit of a bad name because they can have some negative consequences and can be addictive, but did you know gaming skill can translate into physical skill? It has been shown that surgeons who operate using a laparoscope (a viewing tube inserted through a small incision for keyhole surgery) who play a couple of hours of video games each week generally perform better in the operating theatre, making 35 per cent fewer mistakes and completing their tasks 24 per cent faster. For workers operating machinery or intricate tools this could be a distinct advantage. And if any of you are waiting for elective surgery that requires laparoscopy, you know now to ask your potential surgeon how many times they have broken track records at Monterey in *Gran Turismo*.

Why learning really does take AGES

The neuroscience model AGES, devised by Lila Davachi, Tobias Kiefer, David Rock and Lisa Rock, is a great way to ensure the ROI of any training program in the workplace is positive and enduring. To learn anything we have to pay attention to what has to be encoded into our memory bank. We then have to retain the information in the appropriate memory deposit box and finally, the 'pièce de résistance', to be able to access the information at the time it is required.

The AGES model comprises:

Attention

Generation

Emotion

Spacing.

YOUR ATTENTION PLEASE

Focusing our attention in a world of distractions requires more than a request to turn off our phones in class. Providing a learning environment that is as free from distractions as possible can involve taking people off-site to a specified training area and planning the program to incorporate a variety of ways to maintain engagement. This may include storytelling, undertaking pre-reading, experiential activities, games and discussion. Flipped classrooms work by providing the core information prior to attendance, with class time spent on clarifying and deepening understanding. Effective integration of the training in the workplace can happen only where the material is perceived as relevant to the participant themselves and their job or role.

GENERATING MEMORY

Getting information to stick happens when we ascribe meaning and associations using our own insights. That's why sitting passively listening to a lecture is not the best way to learn.

The new way of teaching revolves around driving neuroplasticity, creating new linkages to other neural pathways through a combination of modalities. Memories are not stored in neat filing cabinets; they involve vast networks of interlinked data. The greater the number of associations we form, the easier it is to retrieve the material later.

Repetition has always been a core element of our ability to remember information. It turns out that repetition doesn't work on its own, though.

How many times have you repeated a key piece of information, such as a phone number or address, to find that within a short time it has vanished from your head — *unless* some other associations were made. This might mean structuring the learning to incorporate an element of self-discovery — that is, generating your own learning.

EMOTION IS CRUCIAL TO LEARNING

We make around 30 000 decisions every day, many of which are subconscious and all of which incorporate our emotions. In the business world emotion has been seen as inappropriate because of the belief that when it comes to problem solving and decision making we can and should rely solely on our logic and analysis. This simply isn't true. Our emotions play an important role in all our thoughts and actions. We are moved mainly by emotion, not logic.

The trick is to get the balance right, because we have what neuroscientist Amy Arnsten calls a Goldilocks brain: everything has to be just right. When we are in a positive mood, our mind is more open to learning, to seeing things differently, to considering all options and possibilities. This promotes greater imagination and creativity and helps us to retain what we have learned.

Emotion and memory are very strongly intertwined. That's because in a heightened level of stress our amygdala becomes hyperactive and enhances those memories with a strong emotional component, while activity in the hippocampus, the area of the brain associated with learning and memory, decreases.

SPACING

Cramming doesn't work. Countless students over the ages have denied themselves sleep prior to exams in the mistaken belief that staying up all night might help a couple of extra useful nuggets of information to stick. If anything, it reduces students' potential to get that really high grade because they are already cognitively tired when they start the exam, and they are unlikely to retain any of that extra data in the longer term.

In organisational learning this is not what is desired. Cramming doesn't work, which is where spacing comes in. Rather than trying to condense a three-hour program into 90 minutes (to save time), project managers and trainers are far better off providing short chunks over a longer period of time. This gives the brain a chance to digest and assimilate the information and has been shown to increase retention significantly.

Finding the right spacing balance has been shown to be complex. It does appear that increasing the space gap improves retention because the brain has to work harder to remember it, and it is that increase in effort that strengthens the memory.

Promoting a culture for learning

The authors of the AGES model remind us of the important neurological factors to consider when designing a learning or training program:

» The prefrontal cortex can process between three and seven items of information at any one time, so highlighting a few key points is far more effective than dumping a whole lot of information into one session.

» Learning is a neurobiological process. It takes time to form new synapses.

» New synaptic connections are fragile. It is easy to lose a memory if the synapse is disturbed before it becomes firmly embedded.

» Long-term memory requires brain breaks. This time is needed for consolidation of the information and for the new content to be distributed and organised in the hippocampus.

» Today organisational learning is about developing capacity and capability. It has to provide engagement and meaning.

» As businesses grapple with the problems of staying relevant and competitive, achieving change through acquiring new skills and knowledge requires a workforce to be happy, motivated and engaged.

Any learning program today requires:

» an understanding of where an individual or group is currently at in relation to a skillset

» ensuring the learning is relevant, set at an appropriate level, meaningful and fun!

» providing a clear framework on how to achieve the expected outcomes

» accountability and progress reports

» experiential (where appropriate) and spaced learning to embed the learning

» keeping it brain-friendly with adequate breaks and refueling stops.

Mindfulness
Finding enough thinking space

It's 1854. You've just published a new book called *Walden*, which you feel may have a few years of shelf life in it, if that isn't too immodest. But now it's time to get back to work ... in your other day jobs. As a poet. A philosopher. An abolitionist, naturalist, tax resister, development critic, surveyor and historian. Then, of course, there's your new interest in Hindu and Buddhist scriptures that speak of 'freeing your mind'.

Imagine if Henry David Thoreau were alive today. *On the Duty of Civil Disobedience* would never have been written, because he would have been too focused on social media campaigns, taking down trolls and lambasting the federal government. His brain would now be far too full of the minutiae and 'busyness' of daily struggle to devote time to original thinking.

One thing many of us yearn for is that breathing space that would give us time to think. Whether we are the CEO, manager or solo operator of a high-performance brain, we all seem to have become too busy to give our work the amount of thinking time it deserves.

The consequence of this is that we are selling ourselves short, constraining our ideas and thoughts to the B-class seats in the auditorium of our mind. Yet the one thing that will distinguish us from the also-rans and wannabes is that ability to think carefully and deeply.

One way to achieve this is by adopting a more mindful approach. While mindfulness and different meditation practices are nothing new, their rapid uptake in the corporate world suggests there is something this practice provides us with that helps us manage our crazy busy world more effectively.

Brainy facts about mindfulness

The regular practice of mindfulness has been associated with:

» improving focus and concentration; it helps us prioritise and manage specific tasks and goals

» keeping us in the present moment, the here and now

» reducing stress and alleviating the symptoms of anxiety and depression

» enhancing clarity of thought

» improving decision making

» improving working memory and frontal lobe activity

» providing greater conscious control over our thoughts and ability to respond without judgement

» helping us to see the bigger picture, to broaden our perspective and reduce the emotional attachment we apply to our usual thought filters

» developing greater compassion towards ourselves and others, boosting empathy and relatedness

» a feeling of calmness

» enhancing emotional and physical wellbeing and increasing longevity

» getting better sleep

» reducing sensitivity to pain

» boosting creativity.

Physiological changes are seen on neuroimaging as increased thickness of the grey matter in the prefrontal cortex and hippocampus, and reduction in the size of the amygdala (see figure 8.1).

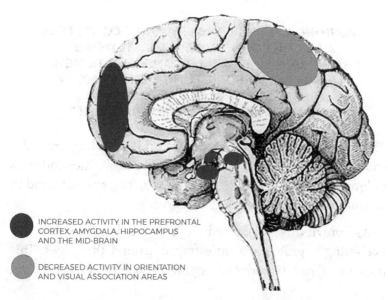

INCREASED ACTIVITY IN THE PREFRONTAL CORTEX, AMYGDALA, HIPPOCAMPUS AND THE MID-BRAIN

DECREASED ACTIVITY IN ORIENTATION AND VISUAL ASSOCIATION AREAS

Figure 8.1: how mindfulness affects the brain

Operating at fast-forward

Lack of thinking time is not just a product of lack of focus. It is a consequence of our super-busy, super-productive working lives, every waking moment of which we have filled to the brim with activity.

As our technology has developed and become increasingly integrated into our lives, so has our love affair with being super-connected 24/7. The downside is that this goes against the grain of how our brain best operates.

Our brain consumes way more energy per unit of mass than the rest of our body (around 20 per cent). The forebrain, the prefrontal cortex, is especially energy hungry, so when our full focus is no longer required, our brain switches automatically to default mode to allow the mighty subconscious to get to work and reduce energy consumption.

PUSHING ON TOO LONG NOT ONLY CONSUMES A LOT OF COGNITIVE ENERGY; IT DENIES THE BRAIN THE TIME TO CONSOLIDATE NEW LEARNING, TO FORM LONG-TERM MEMORY AND START TO MAKE ASSOCIATIONS BETWEEN NEW AND OLDER THOUGHTS.

This is what gives us the depth of understanding around a subject. It allows us to consider different possibilities and ways of looking at challenges. In other words, it opens our mind to alternatives, to new ideas and to learning.

As previously discussed, our super-busy brains are becoming cognitively a little frayed around the edges. This puts us at risk of reduced cognition and increased mental distress. The way to tackle this is to give ourselves permission to slow our brains down. This is rather like the way the Slow Food movement advocates the idea of stepping away from fast foods to reconnect with how we prepare, eat and enjoy real food so we are truly nourished.

In his book *In Praise of Slow*, Carl Honoré talks about how our need for speed has infiltrated everything we do, and his belief that this is detracting from our ability to be fully human.

So what would it be like to choose to dial down our daily run through life? Would that affect how we see our world? Would it influence our behaviours and choices? Would it make us happier?

The answer is yes to all the above, because we can change the way we view the world by taking a broader perspective and noticing more. By opening up our mind to alternatives and possibility thinking we keep consciously engaged with what is happening now, rather than relying on our automatic behaviours.

What's your perspective?

Our own view of the world is unique, shaped by our values, beliefs and experiences. Being aware that not everyone shares our perspective allows us to examine our own filters, our beliefs and biases, at both a conscious and a subconscious level.

Because our conscious mind processes information in a linear way, we will sometimes hold a number of ideas at the front of our mind. This can lead to a bit of a bottleneck and affect how quickly we can work through these thoughts.

While we can hold a couple of ideas simultaneously, we can only 'see' one image at any given moment. This is the basis of optical illusions that provide two representations of an object (see figure 8.2). We have to flick visual channels so as to 'see' the other and this chews up precious mental energy.

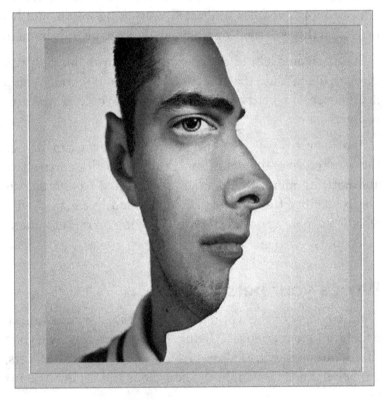

Figure 8.2: optical illusion

To maintain cognitive energy and avoid overloading the prefrontal cortex, we need to reduce the number of complex issues we contemplate at any one time.

Saving brain energy

If brain energy were a fossil fuel, we would be looking to reduce our brainy carbon footprint. There are several strategies that allow us to achieve this.

KISS it

Simplify a complex idea to understand concepts or analogy. In other words, keep it simple, stupid!

Chunk it

Telephone numbers, passwords and other complex strings of digits and numbers can be remembered more easily by chunking them down — preferably into elements that take less than two seconds to repeat to ourselves.

Prioritise it

Identify the most important item on your brain's agenda so as to focus your energy on what needs resolving first.

Mindfulness over matter

Slowing down our mind and broadening our perspective is critical. One way many business leaders and others have discovered to help slow down their brains, and to find the thinking space they seek, has been through adopting a mindful approach to their lives and work.

Mindfulness has become a bit of a buzzword. It's currently all the rage, even though advocates of mindfulness (like our old friend Thoreau) have been practising it for thousands of years.

The reason for its surge in popularity is that it has been shown to be effective in reducing our levels of stress and clarifying our thinking. Some people like to use it as an attention-building tool, others as a means to rediscover a sense of inner calm. What has been especially exciting is the discovery of the effect mindfulness has on our brains, and it's all very good news.

So if you are tempted to dismiss mindfulness as just another passing fad, as a bit woo-woo and one more way to distract yourself from getting your work done, consider this.

MINDFULNESS TAKES US OFF AUTOPILOT. WHEN WE ARE BEING MINDFUL WE ARE FULLY CONSCIOUS OF OUR ENVIRONMENT AND OUR THOUGHTS.

There are now so many recognised cognitive and other benefits from practising mindfulness that we have an embarrassment of good reasons to consider trying it out for ourselves.

People who practise mindfulness have been shown to be more productive, creative, focused, clear thinking, calm, resilient, alert and energised.

In addition, the benefits to our physical health and wellbeing include lower levels of stress, better sleep patterns, and a heightened sense of wellbeing and happiness.

Mindfulness is now being introduced into the corporate world as a way to help employees manage stress levels. As our stress continues to rise like the sea levels, mindfulness has been found to provide an effective way to quieten the chattering mind and restore clarity of thinking. It helps to reduce the hyperactivity of the limbic system and dampens down the stress response.

The only thing required to become more mindful is the decision to learn how. There are a multitude of different meditation practices and no one is better than any other. It all depends on which practice you find works for you. Being curious and open to exploring different practices will help you discover which one best suits your lifestyle and temperament.

Mindfulness is the art of noticing more, especially the new things (people, events, situations and experiences) that constantly pop up in our environment. Novelty is exciting to the brain, but it can also be associated with uncertainty and suspicion. What if it's potentially dangerous and wants to hurt us?

Psychologist Ellen Langer defines mindfulness as 'an active state of mind characterised by drawing novel distinctions' that results in:

» being situated in the present

» being sensitive to context and perspective

» being guided not determined by rules and routine

» full immersion into engagement.

Jon Kabat Zinn, who developed the Mindfulness Based Stress Reduction (MBSR) course in 1979, interprets mindfulness slightly differently as 'paying attention in a particular way: on purpose, in the present moment and non-judgementally'.

THE SECRET IS IN THE NEUROPLASTIC SAUCE

The special sauce in mindfulness is that this and other forms of meditative practice induce neurobiological change. Novices undertaking mindfulness meditation practicing for 30 minutes each day over eight weeks have exhibited a physiological change in their brains that can be measured on MRI scans. The scans show increased cortical density and thickness of the grey matter in the prefrontal cortex, the areas associated with empathy and compassion; and in the hippocampus, the brain area associated with learning and memory (see figure 8.3, overleaf).

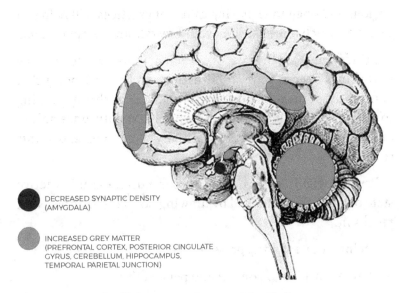

DECREASED SYNAPTIC DENSITY
(AMYGDALA)

INCREASED GREY MATTER
(PREFRONTAL CORTEX, POSTERIOR CINGULATE
GYRUS, CEREBELLUM, HIPPOCAMPUS,
TEMPORAL PARIETAL JUNCTION)

Figure 8.3: mindfulness and neuroplasticity

What this means is that the practice leads to an increase in the number of new synaptic connections being formed. This is neuroplasticity in action.

Even two weeks of practice is enough to make a difference. In another study, novice meditators who were taught a daily 30-minute practice of compassion meditation showed measurable physiological changes in the brain *and* changes in behaviour after just seven hours of practice. Do you see what I see?

**IF IT IS POSSIBLE TO BRING
ABOUT BEHAVIOURAL CHANGE IN SEVEN HOURS,
HOW USEFUL COULD THIS BE TO HELP YOUNG
PEOPLE WITH ANGER MANAGEMENT PROBLEMS,
OR ADULTS WITH POOR EMOTIONAL CONTROL, OR
VIOLENT CRIMINALS WITH SERIOUS BEHAVIOURAL
ISSUES? THE POTENTIAL HERE IS ENORMOUS.**

Of course, deciding to take up mindfulness or any other form of meditative practice remains a personal choice. You can't force anyone to learn meditation if they are resistant to the idea, but mindfulness meditation has already been introduced to address some of these problem areas, to profoundly beneficial effect.

There is a caveat though. Because mindfulness is now so popular, it has been touted as the answer to all our societal ills, which of course it is not. Nor does everyone want to use mindfulness. For those who are interested to give it a try, it can be a very useful tool to assist in managing daily life, reducing the associated stress and anxiety of always feeling 'on' and pushing too hard or too fast.

The best way to incorporate mindfulness in your life is to be taught correctly by an accredited meditation teacher with sufficient experience to be credible.

LIVE LONG AND PROSPER

Meditation affects our longevity through the influence it exerts on our telomeres, structures that sit like shoelace caps on the end of our chromosomes. The telomeres were shown by Elizabeth Blackburn, joint recipient of the Nobel Prize in Physiology in 2009, to protect our chromosomes (and DNA) from degradation.

As part of the aging process, with each cell division our telomeres gradually become shorter until they reach a critical length and the cell dies. Dr Blackburn and her team discovered the enzyme telomerase and showed how it influences the length of our telomeres (see figure 8.4). The researchers found that people who practised regular mindfulness meditation over a four- to six-month period increased the length of their telomeres by 30 per cent.

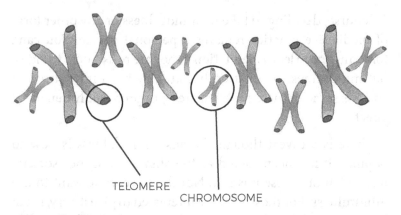

TELOMERE

CHROMOSOME

Figure 8.4: telomeres

Other recent research by Richard Davidson and others has revealed how mindfulness meditation can change gene expression through influencing inflammatory processes.

When we are stressed, our body produces higher levels of cortisol, and a number of pro-inflammatory genes, including RIPK2 and CoX2, become elevated. Mindfulness meditation in more experienced meditators down-regulates these genes, allowing a faster return to full health. The implication here is that meditation may help in *preventing* physical ill health. Now that has to be music to any health professional's ears, and to governments wondering how to cope with spiralling health costs.

Meditation is an easy technique to learn, there are no associated ongoing costs and the potential benefits are enormous.

Team mindful

Lack of engagement remains a thorny issue for many employers, who are racking their brains on how to re-engage their staff. Mindfulness is one component to consider including in a wellness program. Not only does each brain benefit individually, but a mindful business culture enjoys greater organisational health.

Mindfulness for work and living: a case study

Alicia is the CEO and founder of a highly successful small business. She became interested in exploring mindfulness to help her deal with some health issues. A health practitioner described her as a 'highly functioning chaotic person!'

One method she explored was the use of silence. She admits she didn't find this easy. Listening to the silence tape, she thought it was getting stuck as the voice she was listening to stopped speaking. Having tried three times to resolve the loss of sound, the penny dropped that it wasn't that the tape was broken, but that silence had been purposefully included!

Alicia finds her mindful practice makes her feel more productive and better able to switch off. She finds it easier to distinguish what's really important from what can wait, and to handle stressful situations. A chronic insomniac who is often awake at 3 am going through her to-do list, she now uses mindful breathing to get back to sleep more easily.

Taking a mindful approach to her self-care has allowed her to be more self-aware, insightful and perceptive of what is going on around her.

The work culture is now firmly grounded on the values of respecting healthy work practices, including the expectation that everyone stops work by 6 pm at the latest.

MINDFULNESS TAKES A BOW

For those with a job that is enjoyable, exciting and challenging, work is a good place to be. For many people, however, their work is purely a means to pay the bills. Not all work is stimulating and interesting. Boredom stresses the brain and leads to a greater level of distractibility and mind wandering, which in certain instances can put employees at greater risk of injury.

Even highly skilled professionals can get bored. Aging pop stars play to their loyal fans, who naturally want to hear those golden oldies they know and love. But if the artists have been singing the same song for 40 years, you can imagine they are sick to death of it. Trying to make it sound fresh each time must be a challenge.

Mindfulness can play a role here. Ellen Langer did a fascinating study in which she asked symphony players who had been playing the same pieces of classical music for years to play more mindfully. She did this by encouraging some of the players to make their performance feel new in some very small and subtle way. The result? People who heard the mindful players enjoyed the performances more. Langer believes mindful attention to performance leads to greater creativity and charisma and more positive results, whatever the activity being performed.

Being mindful keeps our mind curious and solution-focused.

JOHNNY-COME-LATELY

John has a habit of running late. He doesn't do it deliberately to annoy others; rather, it reflects his attention to detail and his meticulous application to staying on task until a job is done. I know this because we have been married for over 30 years. I like to get to an airport in good time for a flight; John likes to travel closer to the wire. While I stress about being late, he finishes what needs to be done and (usually) still gets to the appointed place in time. His method of working is different from mine. I could choose to get annoyed (okay ... sometimes I do), or I could be more mindful about the situation and keep everyone less stressed.

So what about in your workplace? Do you have a Johnny-come-lately who is consistently the last into the room for team meetings or to turn in work or complete tasks? It's easy to become irritated by their behaviour, and to judge them as being, say, lazy, disorganised or a poor team player.

Taking a mindful approach would be more productive:

» Are they aware of the effect their tardiness has on others?

» Are they late because they are juggling too many other tasks simultaneously?

» Are they having to deal with a crisis at home such as a relationship breakdown or serious illness?

» Are they unhappy in their position, wishing they could work somewhere else?

This would allow you to explore all the possibilities with the person concerned, without judgement or preconceived answers, to facilitate a resolution of the issue.

COMING OFF AUTOPILOT

Mindfulness can help improve our accuracy in recording or remembering important details such as appointments and special dates. Of course using prompts in the form of sticky notes, calendar alerts or a diary can help too. In some instances, checklists are devised specifically for when a complex procedure has to be followed. But there is a caveat.

Checklists work if they are followed and, importantly, used mindfully.

Unfortunately, so much of our behaviour is automatic that we stop noticing what we are doing. For example, one weekend you are driving your car en route to a particular destination, and halfway there you realise you have taken the wrong route because your brain was on autopilot and was taking you to work. Your checklist of 'get in car and drive to destination' didn't include the mindful check-in to ensure you were driving to the *right* destination.

My husband is a pilot and is fanatical about adhering to checklists prior to any take-off and landing. Whilst he has safely taken off and landed hundreds of times, he is acutely aware that his brain is fallible. He knows the checklists play an important role in making up for this natural 'human deficiency' and so help keep everyone safe.

Similarly, in an operating theatre, the surgeon and team will use a series of checklists to ensure the right patient is having the correct procedure, the right side of the body is being operated on, and all instruments and swabs are accounted for.

But even the best checklists in the world can fail us if they are not used mindfully. You may hear the instruction and respond 'Check' because you have heard it a thousand times before, but did you remember to actually flick the switch?

Practice makes peaceful

The essence of freeing your mind from busyness, and giving it room to think, is to make a start — and that involves choosing which form of meditation practice is best for you. The answer is 'the one you like and that best fits your lifestyle'.

Different forms of meditation practice do produce subtle differences in brain outcomes. If focus is your thing, then mindfulness might be the one to try. If your empathy and relatedness need a boost, loving kindness or compassion meditations would be good to try.

It's called a *practice* because it is practised regularly like a musical instrument, ideally every day. Richard Davidson suggests sprinkling several two- to three-minute meditation practices across your day.

Mindfulness, in my mind, produces a ripple effect. My formal daily mindfulness practice then leads to a more mindful approach to other daily activities such as eating, exercising and interacting with others.

HOW LONG SHOULD YOU PRACTICE?

As long as the time you have available. Whether it is 50 minutes or five, what matters is putting in the practice in some form, preferably every day.

That five minutes is still enough. As with many other brain-enhancing activities, it is through repeated practice over a period of time that we get the maximum benefit. Make it a regular practice and it quickly becomes a daily habit. While it's a good idea to practise daily, missing an occasional day doesn't matter.

HOW DO I DO THIS?

When first starting out, it's a good idea to choose a place you can use regularly, somewhere you come to associate with the practice. But of course you can do it anywhere, from a quiet room in your house where the sunlight first enters in the morning, to a park, a mountaintop, a café, even a supermarket queue.

At the start it is probably worth joining a class to help you get into the habit of doing your practice. A class keeps you accountable and you get to meet lots of like-minded people. Classes are typically held weekly over eight weeks, and you can expect to be given homework!

Tuning in to your body and learning how to quieten your mind can be a challenge, especially if you are used to working at a frantic pace. This is where the body scan meditation or some deep breathing exercises can help you feel more relaxed and in tune with your bodily sensations.

The following suggestions for using breathing exercises to aid relaxation could easily be incorporated into your workday. As a manager, team leader or executive, encouraging your staff to participate in some form of regular relaxation practice can be highly beneficial, as it promotes calm, focused thinking and results in a happier, more productive workplace.

This could take the form of a 15- to 20-minute relaxation session at the beginning of the workday or after lunch. Some employers might balk at the prospect of the 'interruption' caused by a staff relaxation session or power nap, but in terms of increased productivity, that 15 minutes of relaxation, meditation or naptime could result in another two to three hours of efficient, high-quality work.

FOCUS ON THE BREATH

If using a floor rug, lie on your back, allow your feet to fall apart, your arms to relax at your sides, palms upturned, and gently close your eyes. If sitting, choose a chair in which you can comfortably place your feet flat on the floor, and tuck your back into the chair so you are not slouched or leaning but sitting upright, as though a cord is gently pulling your head upward. Place your hands in your lap so your arms are relaxed and comfortable, and either gently close your eyes or adopt a soft gaze looking down.

Now focus on your breath. Notice the passage of the air as it enters and leaves your body, the rising and falling of your chest and the contact of your body with the floor or the chair. If you notice your mind wandering off into thoughts or ideas or places (and that does happen, repeatedly!) just acknowledge this and each time gently bring your focus back to your breath.

Mindfulness is not about 'emptying' your mind or falling asleep; it is a mental discipline of focusing on one thing — your breathing — to keep in the here-and-now, the present moment. What happens is that because you are thinking about what is going on right now, you stop thinking about the future or your past; you remain engaged with the present. This skill, built up over time, makes it easier for you to stay on task and to manage your distractions more effectively, more mindfully.

Mindful leadership

Mindfulness is now well established in the corporate world. Since Chade-Meng Tan, Chief Happiness Officer at Google, introduced his Search Inside Yourself program in 2007, many other companies have introduced mindfulness programs, including Aetna, *The Huffington Post*, General Mills, Apple, Medtronic and Goldman Sachs. Companies are funding these programs for their staff and setting up meditation rooms.

Why? Because they have found that offering meditation classes to employees as part of a workplace wellness program can:

» increase productivity

» reduce stress-related illness

» reduce absenteeism

» reduce the incidence of mistakes and errors

» improve recall and memory.

Mindfulness for leadership: a case study

Alison holds a senior management position within a large national company that she describes as being a bit 'old school'. She was aware her whole life had become fast paced and wanted to slow things down, so she took up yoga.

While her yoga helped her sleep pattern, she felt she needed something more. After attending a three-day mindful leadership course, she started to think about how she could incorporate some of what she had learned in to her workplace.

The first step was to hold a leadership forum introducing the 60 participants to yoga and a facilitated introduction to meditation. A far cry from the usual format!

Her team now starts each workday by observing one minute of silence to quieten down the mind and get ready for the day ahead.

A third change has been the inclusion of personal agendas in the annual business plans. The premise is that because everyone is expected to always be operating at their best, it is up to the individual to make the appropriate lifestyle choices to achieve that.

Overall, Alison has found these mindful changes have increased accountability, changed the language being used and built greater capacity. She also reports greater collaboration and more effective teamwork.

Her view is that being mindful is not just something we do for our work or home life; it is for every aspect of our life.

CEOs and leaders such as Ray Dalio, Bill Clinton, Rupert Murdoch, Mark Benioff and the late Steve Jobs have all practiced mindfulness as a way to help them manage their leadership positions more effectively.

Meditation and mindfulness apps such as Headspace encourage people to take 10 minutes out of their day to help improve their health and wellbeing. While mindfulness is commonly used to boost efficiency and productivity, its impact on elevating health and wellbeing cannot be underestimated. A healthy workforce is a happier workforce, which naturally translates into greater engagement, motivation and fulfilment.

Leaders must have the thinking space to pause and reflect. Our current practice of operating continuously at full pelt denies the brain the opportunity to do what it does best — assimilate facts, find new associations and determine the best course of action.

The practice of introspection, using mindfulness or whatever meditation method we find helpful, makes it easier for us to stay connected to what really matters and to let go of the unimportant. As Daniel Goleman, author of *Primal Leadership,* wrote recently, 'a primary task of leadership is to direct attention. To do so leaders must learn to focus on their own attention ... Every leader needs to cultivate the triad of awareness of self, others and the wider world'.

In a world where the pace is continuing to gather momentum, mindfulness offers a means to regain control of our thinking and, by reducing stress, to re-engage with our work and lives in a more meaningful way.

Part III
Integrating a high-performance brain

Change ability
Adjusting to progress

Change management. Change curve. Change request. Change control. Change values. Over the past 30 years a whole industry has been created around — yes, you guessed it — the management of managing change.

The challenge for our brains (and our bodies) as we head into the digi-age is the increasing rate of change, both personal and professional. Just as we get a grip on a new concept in business, there's yet another change in process, procedure or product.

It's fair to say that those who adapt earliest to the latest app rule the world. Understanding how change affects the brain is therefore essential to creating an effective framework for our hardworking neural pathways.

Brainy facts about change and the workplace

» Change never occurs in isolation. If there is a change at work, it invariably affects the whole

(continued)

Brainy facts about change and the workplace *(cont'd)*

organisation (or at the very least a department or section of it).

» Organisational change is one of the major disruptors in business today.

» Most people instinctively think of change as threatening. It is generally seen in negative rather than positive terms. Word of change in the work environment leads quickly to an atmosphere of mistrust, unreliable gossip, division between staff and line management, and a culture of stagnation.

Man overboard

Like evolution, change is a continuum. Think of it as an ocean with rips, ebb tides and currents swirling around constantly. Just as we find our feet or begin treading water furiously with one swell of change, another huge wave comes crashing in and we struggle desperately against being dragged under by a powerful rip that pulls us in a new direction.

So it's essential that we understand this: it's the process of effectively managing change, rather than reaching a static end point, that is our goal and achievement.

OUR BRAINS ARE DESIGNED TO ADAPT CONSTANTLY, NOT REST IN STASIS. SO THAT OCEAN? WE ACTUALLY NEED IT. BUT WE ALSO NEED THE ABILITY TO SWIM WELL, A BACKUP LIFE JACKET, AND A 'WHISTLE AND LIGHT TO ATTRACT ATTENTION'.

Our brains, in other words, need a new approach to make effective change happen on a business level. We have to rethink the way we perceive change and, even more, how we perceive other people's reactions to change. Are they drowning or waving?

Look at change from your brain's point of view and you'll soon see exactly why it's so hard for people to embrace it.

Listen to the screech of the violins just as Norman Bates snatches back that shower curtain in Hitchcock's classic 1960 psychological-horror film. It makes your brain want to hide in the cupboard, and if your body doesn't feel like coming along for the ride, too bad. Hitchcock himself admitted that Bernard Hermann's score created '33 per cent of the effect of *Psycho*'.

In the shower scene that harsh, discordant change in the music spells one thing only to our brains: threat. We instinctively fight change. It's not natural, therefore it's bad, right?

Wrong. Not every change leads to Anthony Perkins with a serious case of the Oedipus blues. Change can be very positive and good for us. We look forward to a holiday or a break from work or even a new role. 'I am so looking forward to a change of routine.' We enjoy a break in the weather or a change of season. We look forward to the arrival of a new baby or an engagement or a wedding.

CHANGE SIGNALS GROWTH, RENEWAL AND OPPORTUNITY. WHAT WE HAVE TO DO IS ENSURE THAT WE KEEP OUR THREAT RESPONSE UNDER CONTROL WHEN IT COMES TO THE CHANGE MANAGEMENT PROCESS AND OUR BRAINS.

That, and do our research on TripAdvisor to choose carefully which motel we decide to check into.

The drama of change

Think of your brain as a TV studio. While we are busy at work, paying attention to our tasks, planning, organising and making decisions, our conscious mind (our prefrontal cortex) is on duty. You could call it the Producer. This part of our brain is metabolically highly active and chews through an enormous amount of energy to get us through our day. It has to make sure the show gets on the air, so to speak.

Meanwhile in the dingy back office, the security guard of the brain, the limbic system incorporating the amygdala, is also on alert. It provides our brain with an automatic alarm to warn us if it recognises we might be in danger.

Much like real TV studio security, because it's a little dark and the TV monitors are a bit grainy, the system picks up a lot of false alarms. The brain doesn't mind, though, because it's *safety first* at all times.

THE BRAIN'S DEFAULT IS INITIALLY TO TREAT ANYTHING NEW IN OUR ENVIRONMENT AS A DANGER.

Those limbic security guards are all about draw first, ask questions later. There'll be plenty of time to check on the validity of the alarm afterwards.

This survival system is responsible in large part for our continuing evolutionary success. In fact, it's perhaps even more significant now than in the past, because our limbic system sees threats everywhere. Why? Because it's triggered by novelty. There weren't a lot of technological changes in Bedrock. Now? We are constantly being introduced to new tasks, people, environments and, of course, digital capabilities.

Back to our scheduled program. Imagine that our Producer—our prefrontal cortex—is busily completing a new script sign-off and at the same time organising the scene set for the evening news. The Security Chief—the anterior cingulate cortex—notes that something new has been picked up on our cerebral screen. This, in turn, alerts the amygdala bovver boys and leads to a cascade of events we know as the stress response.

Simultaneously, the weatherman arrives and hears the alarm go off. He is our emotions, which in this case will have a negative charge—fear, anxiety, uncertainty. The forecast for our business thinking? Not a lot of sunshine.

Fear is the emotion associated with the physiological preparations our body makes before deciding on whether to fight or flee. A racing pulse. Pounding heart. Sweaty skin. Clawing tension in the gut. We ask ourselves what we need to do to stay safe.

In a business context, our brain may make all kinds of rationalisations:

» 'Just ignore it. If we keep a low profile, the boss will choose someone else to present at the monthly meeting.'

» 'Taking on that new role might mean having to move to a different location away from family and friends.'

» 'What were you thinking, putting yourself forward for promotion? You might fail!'

» 'Don't agree to that proposal because it's going to take a lot of work and time you just don't have.'

» 'Don't go there, because others might see you for the impostor you are.'

Worse still, the more active the Security Chief amygdala is, the harder it is to keep control of a situation. Greater limbic activity reduces access to our prefrontal cortex (PFC). So if the Producer isn't in charge, what happens to the show?

Luckily we can use our conscious awareness of what the limbic system is doing and learn to override the threat.

It's not about dismissing the importance of staying safe. It's about using our brain's ability to keep the PFC and limbic system in balance.

THE NEED FOR LONG-LIFE BATTERIES

Another thing to know about our brain in relation to change is that it will do almost anything to conserve energy. This means not expending energy wastefully on thinking tasks that don't warrant it. Instead we package up those thoughts, actions and behaviours into our habits and rituals in the part of the brain known as the basal ganglia. You could perhaps think of it as the newsreader, delivering packages by rote from the TV studio.

This conserves our mental energy and allows us to get on with our daily activities. After all, there are only so many ways to say 'Good evening, and welcome to the news'.

Our brain knows we don't need to waste cognitive energy on paying conscious attention to how we get out of bed, put on our clothes and put the kettle on. We create these habits to let us focus on the more important stuff.

Which is why changing them can be problematic. Our habits serve a purpose, so unless we have a pretty good reason to change, they stay firmly embedded in the basal ganglia (see figure 9.1). Fortunately for us we can, if we know how, effect habit change. Charles Duhigg, author of *The Power of Habit*, advises that to break a habit requires us to recognise the cue and reward linked to the habit, and substitute a new routine.

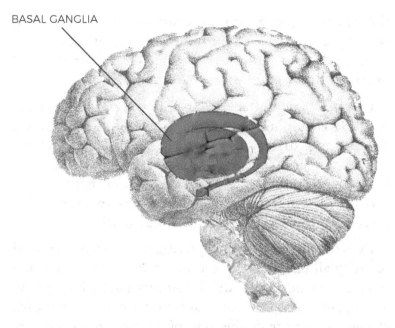

BASAL GANGLIA

Figure 9.1: the brain's habit centre: the basal ganglia

THE SOOTHING BALM OF HABIT

One other benefit that habits confer on our brain is they help to reduce stress. Because habits mostly operate at a subconscious level, we don't pay them much attention so we don't stress about what we are doing. Keeping stress levels down is crucial for successful change.

Changing a habit involves an equation of sorts:

Change = the effort it takes to bring a habit to our level of conscious awareness + the firmness of the decision to change that habit.

This is crucial because if we fail to give ourselves permission to change, it won't happen, and we multiply our brain's inability to cope with change.

When it comes to behavioural change, what we are really asking our brain to do is to consider something new (a huge threat) and to put in the time, effort and practice for a new way of doing. We are asking our brain to create new neural pathways that will ultimately become the preferred way of operating — until the next change comes along.

In 1995 John Kotter, a Harvard professor and leading expert in change management, reported the average success rate of change strategy as around 30 per cent. Since that time, innumerable books about change management and programs have been produced. In 2010 a review in *McKinsey Quarterly* examining what progress had been made to increase the success rate revealed that the answer was none!

Does this mean we are highly resistant to change and should probably all just go home and forget about it? No, because change is essential as an adaptive process that leads to growth and opportunity. We need to examine how we approach change, and we can do this more effectively today because of what has been learned about the neuroscience of change.

As we've already discussed, we are in a world that is moving ever faster, adapting more and more rapidly to new technology, systems and production methods. We exchange information and news in a matter of seconds with just a few keystrokes. The need is not just to keep abreast of change but to know how to lead effective change, and to thrive.

The problem with change

The biggest obstacle to change is — you guessed it — us. We are our own worst enemies. Our brains and our bodies conspire to make change the worst thing since ... well, imagine the very worst thing you can think of, and that's what change is like.

»   It's *tiring*. It requires that the brain use a lot of mental energy.

»   It's *hard work*. It needs a great deal of effort.

» It can be *hard to achieve*. Yes, it's difficult to imagine, but not everyone is going to share your vision for change.

» It can be *scary*. We are very good at frightening ourselves with the prospect of failure, or even success and the uncertainty that brings.

» It can be *lonely*. Initiating change can make us feel isolated unless others support us in our quest.

» It can actually be *'wrong'*. Sometimes our great idea turns out not to be so great, in fact maybe a terrible mistake. Change always includes an element of risk.

Given all these reasons why change is problematic, it's vital to remind ourselves of the benefits change can bring to ourselves and to others:

» *personal growth*. Overcoming the challenges of change brings a sense of achievement and expands our thinking about our capabilities, confidence and competence.

» *flexibility*. Being adaptable creates greater mental flexibility to handle ongoing change. As the pace of change continues to ramp up, having the flexibility to adapt rapidly to new environments, situations and challenges when things turn to custard is a huge advantage.

» *broadening perspective*. We create our reality through the filters of our perception. If we never check that we are using the right lens on our camera, the images we produce may be out of focus or washed out or miss the target completely. Keeping a wide-angle lens on means we can keep sight of the bigger picture and take in all possible variations and alternatives.

Being flexible means being adaptive and supple and engaging fully in the process. Part of that is ensuring there are no unnecessary obstacles in our way. As with distractions, these come in external and internal forms.

EXTERNAL OBSTACLES TO CHANGE

These include people, such as your family, friends and colleagues. They may be concerned for your safety and welfare. They don't want to see you get hurt so they actively discourage you from attempting risky change.

Others, of course, will have their own agenda on why they may not wish you to succeed. Perhaps they feel threatened. If you are successful in losing weight, or giving up smoking or alcohol, or taking up some form of exercise, they may feel bad about themselves.

Families, kids, partners can all have expectations of what normal family life and routine entails, and if the changes you want are likely to impact on them, they may resist. Be aware of this and understand that not all external obstacles are within our control.

INTERNAL OBSTACLES TO CHANGE

This is where how we think and our brain fitness come into play. Things to consider here include mindset and willpower, expectations (of others and ours of ourselves), biases, beliefs, emotion and mood.

Having that brilliant idea can get us all revved up. We can see what a brilliant solution it is. If everyone were to adopt our great idea, we could change the world.

So the day comes when you get to present Your Brilliant New Idea. You've written the presentation, drawn up lots of models, spoken enthusiastically about all the benefits and showcased the Idea.

Except it doesn't bring the reaction you expected. In fact, it falls completely flat. Your colleagues aren't the slightest bit impressed by your rhetoric and examples of how it could work so brilliantly. They don't buy it at all. How can that be? How can they possibly refute all your careful arguments that together create such a compelling and convincing case?

Like any well-prepared negotiator, you will have to demonstrate to your colleagues what's in it for them and how your idea will not cause harm or lead to potential danger.

You will face these internal obstacles. If you don't want to be paralysed by them, a mentor, coach or buddy can provide you with the social support you need to persevere.

Project change

All change is different, but the basic factors that contribute to successful change strategy are the same.

Having made the decision that a change is needed, desired and possible, and having granted yourself permission to change, you're ready to take the first steps.

ABOVE ALL ELSE, KNOW YOUR WHY

Communicating clearly *why* the change is needed and desirable, and the benefit it will bring to those affected, will convince people to buy into the idea. Once all stakeholders feel they have joint ownership of the proposed changes, they will help get the change implemented. In his book *Start With Why*, Simon Sinek talks about how knowing our why in business, work or life is what matters, not what we do.

When Peter Baines, a former police forensic specialist from New South Wales, found himself in Thailand following the Boxing Day tsunami in 2004 to help with victim identification, he realised that there was a generation of orphaned children left homeless with no one to care for them. His why was to establish the charity organisation Hands Across the Water to make a difference to the lives of those kids.

There are many charities that do amazing work for others. What makes Peter's charity stand out from the crowd is that rather than just telling others *what* they do, the story is all about *why* this organisation makes a difference.

SHARE THE VISION

The change leader, or introducer of the idea, has to paint a picture of the future that is BIG, BOLD and CLEAR. Clarity removes confusion and fear, and helps to establish trust and certainty.

The message has to be articulated clearly, openly and repeatedly. Providing a platform for reflection gives people space to consider how the change will impact them and help the company or business.

The online shoe company Zappos has become the poster child for change management. Today Zappos is known as much for its tagline 'Delivering Happiness' as for its shoes. The company has 10 core values that it lives, eats and breathes by:

» Deliver WOW through service.

» Embrace and deliver change.

» Create fun and a little weirdness.

» Be adventurous, creative and open minded.

» Pursue growth and learning.

» Build open and honest relationships with communication.

» Build a positive team and family spirit.

» Do more with less.

» Be passionate and determined.

» Be humble.

The transparency and clarity of the message has contributed to making Zappos a highly desirable place to work. The company's continuing success owes much to the culture that has evolved through the transparency and authenticity of the vision created by its leaders.

MAKE THE CHANGE FRAMEWORK COMMERCIALLY COLLABORATIVE

No one will help the change process if it is seen as too hard. When an architect works with a client, they draft a plan of the house that the client wants, that the builder is capable of building and that council will agree is environmentally acceptable. So it is for the change leader. It's about putting together the right team to work together, which takes the pressure off an individual and spreads the load.

TAKE THE FIRST STEP, THEN THE NEXT

You have worked out the framework complete with timeline and expected implementation dates. No change will be successful until the plan is implemented, but do it in stages. By chunking down the change into smaller pieces, any associated threats are reduced.

As with any meal, whether you are about to eat an elephant or a hamster, it all starts with that first bite, and it is consumed one bite at a time. Savouring that meal slowly allows us to enjoy the positives along the way.

CREATE CO-OWNERS OF THE IDEA

Back to Zappos as an example of how the transparency and clarity of the message contributes to making it a highly desirable place to work. The company's continuing success owes much to the culture that has evolved whereby employees care so much about 'delivering happiness' that they go out of their way to make it happen.

Zappos has abolished the corporate hierarchy, so everyone in the company has an equal voice. Everyone feels safe to give their opinion or share ideas that might benefit their workmates, the company or their customers. If others agree, they lend their support.

At work, hearing praise from a trusted colleague about another person and their ideas offers us the social proof we may need to be persuaded to join in the fun. Co-owners of an idea are worth their weight in gold.

CELEBRATE PROGRESS ALONG THE WAY

Progress towards change needs to be visible, reportable, measurable and celebrated. The greatest motivators of change are not incentives, bonuses or positive feedback (though they can help). The successful progress of the project gives the greatest satisfaction.

STAY FLEXIBLE

Change itself can change. The initial desired outcome may, on later review, require tweaking, reworking or even abandoning. The final goal always needs to remain flexible.

Adopting a culture of change

Reinforcing change requires mental flexibility and a constant awareness of how our own cognitive biases can influence our thinking.

At both an individual and organisational level, developing change ability is key to how we deal with ongoing change in the future. We can use brain science to shift our perspective on how we view potential change and implement effective change strategies.

Change is a two-way street, so change management is about learning how to reduce the threat state that change induces, and regulating the emotional response in ourselves and others.

Change is also all about how people feel. Conversations about change may be difficult and require courage. However hard, it is these conversations that help shift people into a 'towards' state of change acceptance and buy-in.

Walter McFarland points out that change is never linear and sequential; it is non-linear and chaotic. Managing change enables us to move in the direction of our choice.

While the pace of change can feel overwhelming, rapid change is nothing new. As we continue to adapt and evolve, this apparent craziness will feel less overwhelming when we see how we can choose our response. Instead of being panicked into outright rejection or paralysed by fear into inaction, we have the option of considering those ways that will enable an appropriate and timely shift in our behaviour to allow the change to develop.

Change is good: It drives growth and innovation, and it expands our thinking. Times are changing, so our brains need to change and adapt too.

KEY 10
Innovation
Curiosity leads to insight and innovation

Do you remember watching the movie *I, Robot* (or for the Asimov enthusiasts among us, reading the original novel) and thinking, 'That's so far out of our purview it's ridiculous'? What about *Gattaca*, or for that matter *The Matrix*? In reality, each of these movies contains aspects of our 'brave new world' that have become a part of the everyday 'meh'.

As we move further into the digi-age, the rapidity of technological innovation and intuitive design is increasing at an almost unthinkable pace. While these additions to our app shelf will undoubtedly contribute to our rapid adaptation and ability to keep connected and above all to cope, it will be our own mental flexibility, the ability to solve problems quickly and to come up with new ideas, that will be most valuable for our future selves.

IT WILL BE HOW WELL WE CAN INNOVATE AND CREATE – OR LEAD OTHERS TO PERFORM THIS FUNCTION – THAT WILL MATTER THE MOST IN BUSINESS CURRENCY.

Insight is a highly valued cognitive ability. A higher level of insight will differentiate the great from the good and provide the crucial competitive edge in the future.

Brainy facts about innovative and insightful workplace thinking

» The human brain is functionally divided into hemispheres, but uses them both equally to provide us with a complete view of our world.

» Insight is the ability of the brain to form a new, unique association between two or more previously unlinked things or concepts. Think, for example, of putting a strange-looking, grumpy cat into a meme, and setting it loose on the internet. This is (neuro)plasticity — and making a fortune — in action. The moment of insight occurs at the time of the creation of a new synaptic pathway.

» Creativity can be fostered in the right environment — one that encourages inward reflection and an uncoupling from our focused attention. Watching a mindless TV show about bad-tempered people in an IT department while petting your weird-looking cat? Creative gold.

» The brain has two possible pathways to solving problems: insight and logic. Mental flexibility is the ability to alternate rapidly between the two, depending on which route the brain thinks will work best for a given challenge.

Whole-brain thinking

There is no right brain, left brain. While it has been popular to consider ourselves as being controlled by one or the other, there is no scientific basis for this. We use the whole brain to think.

We are all whole-brain creators. So what are the distinctions between the two hemispheres joined together by the corpus callosum?

The main difference, as described by Robert Ornstein, is that 'the right brain hemisphere provides the context. The left hemisphere keeps tracks of the details' (see figure 10.1).

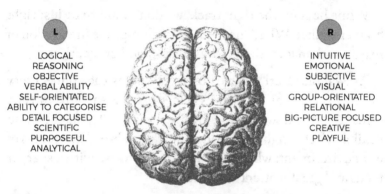

Figure 10.1: functions of left and right hemispheres

Iain McGilchrist, in his book *The Master and His Emissary: The Divided Brain and the Making of the Western World*, suggests the function of the corpus callosum is to keep the two hemispheres apart, to allow each side of the brain to incubate those ideas necessary for the components of divergent thought required for creativity.

He quotes Einstein that 'the intuitive mind is a sacred gift and the rational mind is a faithful servant' while arguing that we have created a society that honours the servant but has forgotten the gift.

What McGilchrist is implying here is that we have progressively early-adopted using our more logical and analytical thinking directed from the left hemisphere but diminished our capacity for creative thought.

Dan Pink, author of *A Whole New Mind: Why Right Brainers Will Rule the Future*, takes this one step further to argue that 'our focus on facts, programming and numbers has led to a devaluing of skills that are often the strengths of the emotionally sensitive, making meaning, consoling, caretaking, awareness of undercurrent in interpersonal interactions and creativity'.

While he is on the right track, we don't want to be just right brainers either. What's needed is the appropriate integration of reason and imagination so they work together seamlessly.

As Szabolcs Keri reminds us, 'creativity is the connectivity of large scale brain networks. How brain areas talk to each other is critical when it comes to originality, fluency and flexibility'. Our right hemisphere sustains a broad awareness of our environment, while the left is more precise with a sharper focus and greater attention to detail.

The problem is that our education system still favours and rewards academic achievement based on measurable applications of logic, memory and reason above creativity. One outspoken critic of the education system, Sir Ken Robinson, believes our innate sense of creativity is knocked out of us by the school curriculum. He sees education as a major global challenge to adequately preparing our future thinkers.

It should seem obvious that our ability to think outside the square and come up with new ideas is going to matter far more than merely having access to data. Many believe the information superhighway could still do with a few more underpasses, several more lanes and at least three new roundabouts.

TYPE CREATIVE

Think of the stereotype of the neurotic *artiste*, flinging a bottle at the dressing-room mirror, demanding a bath filled with asses' milk and that everyone pray to Zuul prior to performances lest the god be offended. Of course, the whole image of histrionic outbursts and psychotic behaviour by 'creatives' is grossly unfair and wrong; however, the brain science does suggest there is a link between creativity and mental health.

Researchers from the Karolinska Institute in Sweden have shown how the dopamine system (the brain's reward system) in highly creative people such as writers, artists and musicians is very similar to that seen in people with schizophrenia. Both have fewer dopamine receptors in the area of the brain called the thalamus, which acts as a kind of relay centre filtering information before it reaches our conscious awareness.

It's thought that having fewer of these receptors could explain why the mechanism in those who are highly creative can identify many more uncommon associations when problem solving — and why those with mental illness sometimes make bizarre associations. It comes down to the level of filtering being applied.

As Dr Ullen, leader of the study, said 'Thinking outside the box might be facilitated by having a somewhat less intact box'.

It's very important to note here that being creative does *not* imply you are at risk of mental illness. You do not have to be mentally ill to be creative, and you do not have to be creative to develop mental illness.

Indeed the act of creativity is generally associated with feelings of happiness, personal growth and wellbeing. Scott Barry Kaufman, Scientific Director of the Imagination Institute, reporting on the findings of another Swedish study, notes that the siblings of people with autism, and first-degree relatives of people with schizophrenia, bipolar disorder and anorexia, appear to be over-represented in creative professions. He concludes that 'mental illness is conducive to creativity *indirectly* by enabling the relatives of those afflicted [with it] to open the mental flood gates, but maintain the protective factors necessary to steer the chaotic, potentially creative storm'.

ALL THAT JAZZ

It was during a trip to New Orleans that I first got to experience musicality at its most primal. We were in a dark, smoky club listening to collective improvised jazz at its finest. Captivated, we listened in awe, trying to anticipate what might be coming next and delighting in the fluidity of musical exchange between the players.

Neuroscientists who have used brain scans to study the brains of jazz musicians were able to observe multiple areas of the brain being activated during this type of improvisation.

Studies from Finland by Oikkonen and others assessing musical creativity discovered a cluster of genes associated with higher musical creativity. It appears that these genes are associated with higher levels of serotonin, which increases connectivity (plasticity) in the area of the brain called the posterior cingulate cortex (PCC) and higher levels of creativity.

In addition, work by neuroscientist and musician Daniel Levitin reveals how music influences our health through neurochemical change in our sense of reward, motivation and arousal, stress levels, immune system and social affiliation.

Perhaps you have used music as a way to soothe an overbusy mind, relieve anxiety or tension, and unwind. Or do you listen to music to put your brain into a relaxed state so you can start thinking in a more creative, non-focused way?

Creativity boosts confidence in our ability to develop new skills as well as broadening our interests.

Having the right environment and encouragement plays a part in how willing we are to be creative. Of course growing up in a family that encourages creative expression will have an impact that is different from what would be experienced growing up in a household where creativity plays second fiddle to academic achievement or is simply considered irrelevant. But regardless of our upbringing, our marvellous plastic brain gives us all the capacity to develop our creative side.

Aha! So that's what insight is all about

The *Oxford Dictionary* defines insight as 'the capacity to gain an accurate and deep understanding of someone or something', from the Middle English for 'inner sight' or 'wisdom'. But insights don't pop up automatically. Sometimes they need to be coaxed, cajoled or teased out.

Our understanding about how insight is generated owes much to the work of Jung-Beeman and Kounios. They began by studying the five distinctive electrical waveforms of brain wave activity that occur depending on whether we are awake, alert or asleep (see figure 10.2, overleaf).

» Delta waves (0–4 Hz) are associated with deep sleep.

» Theta waves (4–7 Hz) occur when we are in a drowsy state, such as when meditating.

» Alpha waves (8–13 Hz) provide the dominant rhythm of the brain at rest. These waves are associated with relaxation and help 'gate' neural activity, reducing visual input processing to help eliminate distractions.

» Beta waves (13–40 Hz) occur when we are in an alert state and increase when we are anxious. Beta activity in the visual cortex correlates with visual focus.

» Gamma waves (30–100 Hz) synchronise especially when we pay attention.

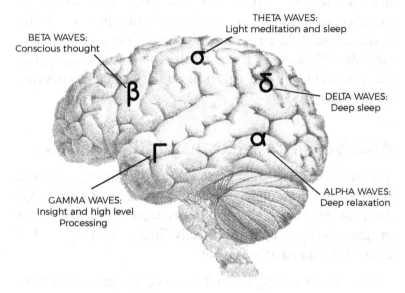

THETA WAVES:
Light meditation and sleep

BETA WAVES:
Conscious thought

DELTA WAVES:
Deep sleep

ALPHA WAVES:
Deep relaxation

GAMMA WAVES:
Insight and high level
Processing

Figure 10.2: brain waves

So what happens in the brain when we create insight? Far from being random, insight follows a process.

It is a right hemisphere activity. When we are preparing to solve a problem with insight we direct our attention to be less focused and more inward looking (reflective). The brain area called the anterior cingulate cortex (ACC) is activated. The ACC acts to detect errors or differences in our environment. As already mentioned, it is involved in cognitive control and attention. This may include the brain preparing to monitor competing responses to the problem and to assist in shifting mental processing to multiple trains of thought.

As the moment of insight draws closer, alpha wave activity in the visual cortex increases, dampening down visual distraction, just as some people will close their eyes when searching for an answer.

A third of a second before the Eureka moment, a peak of gamma wave activity sweeps across the right anterior, superior temporal gyrus. This is the birth of a new idea, when a set of neurons binds or wires together uniquely for the first time, before emerging into our consciousness as the solution.

The bliss of insight is that when it occurs it is sudden and complete, as if the answer was sitting there all along just waiting to be noticed. We have that all-encompassing certainty that we are looking straight at the answer.

Better still, studies by Wills and others show that we remember insightful solutions better because of heightened activity in the hippocampus (the area used to form and retrieve memories) that happens at the same time.

FLEXIBLE THINKING AND PROBLEM SOLVING

Insight is one approach we use to solve problems. The other? Our left brain–dominant use of logic and analysis. We tend towards a natural preference for one approach over the other. Engineers are more likely to approach a problem from an analytical perspective. (I can confirm this as my husband is also an engineer.)

The difficulty here is that because the prefrontal cortex has limited capacity, you can hold only two or three complex ideas front of mind at any one time, and even this consumes a great deal of cognitive energy. It doesn't take long before cognitive exhaustion kicks in, and the likelihood of resolving the problem just packed its bag and walked out of the room, booked a taxi and went to the nearest day spa. Forging on at this point is pretty futile as increasing levels of cognitive fatigue further reduce processing speed and power.

How do you deal with your mental impasses? Do you have another cup of coffee or three? Or do you branch out into gathering further information or brainstorming ideas with others?

The alternative method is to use insight. The advantage here is that, being a primarily subconscious process, it is far less energy-consuming and the enormous capacity of the subconscious mind provides a much larger cupboard to delve into to look for new thought associations.

What is fascinating is that our brain predetermines which route is most likely to come up with the solution and guides us towards that route (which is fine if we are paying attention to our brain's signals).

We are influenced by other factors too. They may include:

» pressure from work colleagues waiting for your contribution before they add their input

» your boss screaming at you because they wanted the problem fixed yesterday

» other external pressures that make you feel tired or anxious.

None of these factors are conducive to effective problem solving, especially creative or insightful problem solving.

So how do you know which method you use to solve problems?

GETTING INTO RATS

No, this isn't another of those experiments using our verminous furry friends. Working with a test for creativity initially devised by Mednick back in 1962, Jung-Beeman and others produced their own version, called the Compound Remote Associates Test, to determine whether you use analysis or insight to solve a problem.

In this test you are asked to look at three words and then come up with a single-solution word to form a common compound word or two-word phrase. Try it, allowing yourself around 30 seconds to come up with your answer.

Here are three words:

HAT, CHOCOLATE, TOOL

(The solution is BOX: *hatbox, chocolate box, toolbox.*)

Too easy? Try another set.

STORM, WAVE, DRAIN

(The solution is BRAIN: *brainstorm, brain wave, brain drain.*)

Which brain method did you use? If you applied logic and analysis, you may have tried a couple of different possibilities before settling on the one word that fitted best? This is *left brain dominance*. If the answer came to you immediately and seemed obvious, you were using insight. This is *right brain dominance*.

Does it matter which route we use?

No. What matters is to develop the mental flexibility to use one or both methods as most appropriate to a particular task.

Solving a problem with insight may follow contemplation and thinking around an issue that has been hanging around for a while, but sometimes insight can occur even when we are under duress. Having the skill to quieten the mind at 'fight or flight' moments can provide an opportunity for the subconscious to come up with a possible solution.

Insight under pressure

While insight more typically occurs when we are unfocused and quietly reflecting inwardly, there are times when extreme circumstances can lead to an answer.

On 5 August 1949 a team of 15 smoke jumpers were parachuted into the area of Mann Gulch in Helena National Park, Montana. Wagner Dodge headed the team. Within two hours of landing, conditions became perilous. The fire was out of control and Wagner ordered his men to drop their heavy packs and run up the side of the gulch to try to escape the fire. Realising that they couldn't outrun the fire, Wagner suddenly had the idea of stopping to ignite a small patch of grass in front of him and to lie down on the smouldering embers. He survived, but 13 other firefighters died that day.

Wagner Dodge intuitively knew that unless he did something different, he would die. Intuition on its own isn't enough, though. He had years of experience in fighting fires and knew that fires depend on fuel and oxygen. His neural insight used that knowledge to come up with the novel solution of removing the fuel and relying on the thin layer of oxygen available to him at ground level as he lay face down and let the fire pass over him.

Wagner used a moment of mental impasse to come up with an insight that offered a possible solution to a seemingly impossible situation, and it bought him his life.

JOINING THE DOTS

Where do you come up with your best ideas? Is it as you wake up in the morning? Is it during an exercise session, while walking on the beach, following the black line in the swimming pool or in the shower? Wherever it is, it's unlikely to be while sitting focusing hard at work.

Creativity is really about joining the dots.

Figure 10.3 depicts a well-known puzzle: nine dots are arranged in a square. The challenge is to connect all of the dots using four straight lines, without lifting your pen from the paper or passing through any dot more than once? Figure 10.4 (overleaf) shows the solution.

Figure 10.3: the nine dots puzzle

This brainteaser is a simple example of when an answer can be found only by thinking in a different way — outside the box.

Our brain is much like some teenagers who would prefer to take the easy route than put in the extra effort to find a new way. It's energy saving for the brain, and the brain sure likes to conserve energy. When presented with a puzzle like this we automatically look for a quick solution, except that doesn't work here.

It takes more effort to push past our 'usual way of doing things' to explore how an unexpected or previously unexplored approach might produce the answer. Once found, that extra effort of working it out produces a much stronger association for your brain to use in its repertoire next time you face a similar challenge.

Practicing brainteasers like these is a great way to develop 'out of the box' thinking and help prepare you for when you face a seemingly impossible challenge in the workplace. They keep you solution focused and open to the possibility of exploring all options and alternatives. Figure 10.4 shows the solution.

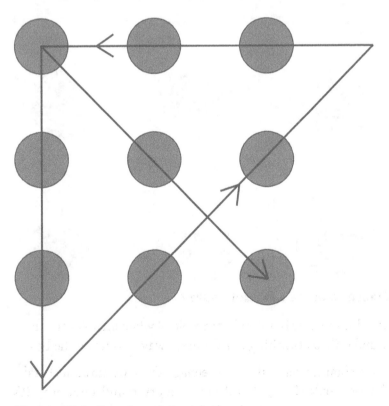

Figure 10.4: the nine dots solution

As with all good brainteasers, once you know the solution it seems so obvious! How did you go with it? Did you try a number of different approaches to see what worked? Did you get frustrated by not being able to solve it? If you did work out the answer, your success probably came about through discarding the 'expected' way of solving the problem.

Looking outside our known area of expertise allows us to expand our thinking and deepen our understanding. So if you see something on a topic that you don't know much about but that piques your interest, explore it and see if new connections start to pop up. Creativity is the ability to connect disparate thoughts and ideas and put them together in a novel way. Which begs the question, is there such a thing as a completely original idea? Maybe all our original ideas are actually no more than compilations of known elements put together in new relationships that haven't been thought of before.

Free-range thinking

Free-range chickens are much happier egg layers, being able to wander about freely with plenty of space. Human minds are much the same.

If your workplace constrains innovative thinking because it prioritises process and conformity, it could reflect the nature of the work required or the timeless 'that's the way things are done around here' mindset. And let's face it, many jobs do require conformity to standards and rules, both for a consistent product and for safety reasons.

But if your work is of the sort where thinking and curiosity could improve efficiency and productivity, then feeling safe to voice your ideas, and having them heard or acknowledged without fear of putdown or ridicule, is a first step towards a more innovative outlook. That's because a brain that feels safe feels relaxed and can access the prefrontal cortex more easily, and feels free to mind-wander as well.

A great example of free-range thinking is offered by the Australian enterprise software company Atlassian. From day one, the founders of the company recognised they needed continuous innovation to develop and build the company successfully. The challenge was how to achieve this on a consistent basis, so they introduced ShipIt Day (formerly known as FedEx Day), a quarterly 24-hour period made available to all employees.

The rule of the game is that all staff have a 24-hour period to work on something related to Atlassian products that they wouldn't be working on normally, but something they have wanted to investigate — an idea they have wanted to develop, a passion, some area where they want to see change. At the end of the 24 hours all ideas are pitched in a show-and-tell and voted on. The winner gets to take home a trophy and a limited edition T-shirt, and there's a beer party to celebrate all efforts.

The success of this initiative has seen other companies around the world who also depend on a high level of creativity adopt similar programs.

TIME OUT FOR THOUGHT

One reason why so many companies struggle with innovation in the workplace is we are all too busy. Busy people are working hard all ... day ... long. It seems like there is never the time to allocate to innovation, even where it is encouraged. New ideas take time to explore and consider. Coming up with a list of bullet-point suggestions isn't innovation. Ideas need to be fleshed out, explored, refined, developed or discarded.

Wise companies that need to encourage more creative thinking schedule in down time for regular brain breaks to allow the mighty subconscious some room to breathe. But just putting a beanbag in a room with some subdued lighting isn't necessarily going to work, because creativity can't be ordered off the menu like a pizza.

SOCIETY AND SENSIBILITY

What is the prevailing mood at your workplace? If staff morale is low, this is a big red danger sign and there is little prospect of innovation. While it's nonsense to insist on staff being 'happy', having the social sensitivity to recognise when someone is unhappy and to *do something about it* is an obvious first line to address.

Being in a bad mood reduces concentration and willingness to engage in out-of-the-box thinking. Emotions are highly contagious, and all it takes is one disgruntled employee or staff member to reduce creative thinking across an entire department or team.

Happiness comes from doing work we find stimulating and rewarding. How we view our work will have a huge impact on how we approach our tasks, trials and challenges. Boosting our mood can be as simple as sharing a joke, watching some comedy and having a good laugh, because this reduces stress and tension and promotes whole-brain thinking.

Having a positive affect or mood matters for creativity because it:

» enhances your awareness of alternative options

» makes it easier for you to switch between different strategies or approaches

» makes it easier for you to make the most appropriate selection at that time.

Anxious staff solve fewer problems with insight compared with those in a more positive mood, who not only solve more problems overall but do so with a greater degree of insight.

INNOVATION IN A FLUX

Fluctuations in attention will occur because of:

» the nature of the work and how much interest it holds for us; it's harder to maintain attention on something we find boring

» our level of fatigue; cognitive fatigue due to lack of sleep or poor quality of sleep will greatly diminish our ability to stay focused and increase the risk of errors.

A tired or bored brain is a stressed brain and far less able to innovate.

It's about recognising individual variations in resting-state brain activity. If your mind is constantly on the go, you might be a PFC rally driver, looking to resolve problems and challenges with your logic or analysis. You might be known as 'the creator', your mind constantly buzzing with new ideas. The buzz alone isn't enough, of course; you have to capture the ideas and design a plan to implement them effectively.

Other brains operate best in a calmer state with a higher level of alpha waves. People who practise regular meditation have been shown to be more insightful, because it becomes easier to drop into a calmer mind that is more conducive to accessing our subconscious thoughts.

Creativity requires focus. It's important to know you are looking at the problem that needs solving. Once you are clear about that, opening up to consider options and possibilities becomes easier.

David Perkins, author of *The Eureka Effect*, suggests 'we are unlikely to achieve insight unless we have struggled with the problem some'. He's right. Those flashes of inspiration don't come from nowhere without previous consideration and forethought. Even then there is no guarantee that the right answer will reveal itself. However, getting enough sleep, keeping stress levels tuned down and remaining curious all help keep the brain in an optimal state for best performance.

CREATIVITY ON THE MOVE

Aerobic exercise boosts our brain's plasticity. It enhances neurogenesis, the production of new neurons, and facilitates the interaction between our PFC and amygdala. Tamping down the amygdala reduces symptoms of stress and anxiety. Exercise boosts our mood, which is great for creativity.

A study by Blanchette and others in 2005 showed how creative potential is increased immediately by aerobic exercise (and for two hours following it). Studies from the Netherlands have also reported that regular exercise acts as a cognitive enhancer of creativity.

It's brainstorming? Quick, get in out of the nasty weather!

Have you ever been in a workshop where the facilitator suggests you spend the next 30 minutes brainstorming for new ideas (then slopes off for a quiet cigarette and a cup of coffee)? I have, and more often than not the activity failed to deliver on its promise.

Despite research indicating that brainstorming isn't always an effective way to produce great ideas, it continues to be promoted in many workplaces confounded by falling sales or productivity.

'I think we should brainstorm the lack of visitors to the website.'

'Er... we could just put some new products on there. The ones we have up currently haven't been in stock for five months.'

'Yes! Brainstorming, that's the key. I'll grab the whiteboard, you get the butcher paper.'

It sounds as if it ought to work. Getting a group of enthusiastic like-minded people together to come up with new ideas should be a breeze, except it doesn't work. Brainstorming is a technique that has been around since 1953 — and was disproved five years later by Yale researchers who found that brainstorming diminished the creative output of a team. Yet the myth (like that of multitasking) has persisted despite all contrary evidence.

Yes, brainstorming will produce new ideas that can be quickly written up on large sheets of butcher paper, but there are problems:

» You can end up with a whole barrel full of less-than-useful ideas, and possibly a few of those typewriter-crazy monkeys. This is a waste of time and effort because it is the quality of ideas, rather than their quantity, that matters. Pooling too many ideas means it can then be difficult to pick out the really good ones.

» Sometimes there is one voice in the group that is louder and more persistent than the others. This can interfere with our own thoughts, which may have been moving in a different direction. Once someone else's big idea is upfront it tends to swamp our own ideas.

» If the vocal person's idea is taken up by the group, other ideas that might be even better are sidelined or not considered any further, whether through fear, laziness, a sense of needing to keep the peace or plain old boredom.

» Feeling pressured to come up with an idea in front of others limits innovative thinking and forces the brain to use more logic and analysis, prefrontal cortical activity that is very energy intensive and quickly exhausting. The need for group harmony overrides the ability to come up with anything useful, with the result that the brainstorming shuts down the thinking processes of the group.

Charlan Nemeth from UCLA found that a 20-minute brainstorming session typically produced an average of three new ideas, compared with seven from a 20-minute focused discussion group.

Skilled debaters develop the art of being able to defend or deconstruct another person's argument or idea. Far from being an aggressive technique, this kind of debate provides the perfect opportunity for those engaged to think more deeply around the issue and to formulate their own opinions.

Overall, debate and critique have been shown to produce more high-quality ideas in a group setting, increasing the average number of new ideas by up to 20 per cent. The greater engagement with the task may provoke more argument or disagreement, but it results in a better outcome.

It's like playing Scrabble: you may see a quick and easy word you can add, but the challenge is to think harder and find a better answer that will score more points.

Is there ever a place for brainstorming? Yes, if directed appropriately:

1. Allow individuals to brainstorm alone first.

2. Then bring the group together to collectively identify which ideas address the problem best and set up a shortlist of those deserving of further thought and attention.

3. Encourage group discussion to debate the pros and cons of any proposed ideas and polish them up ready to answer the question, 'Will this solve the problem we are addressing?'

For the individual: creativity 101

If we adopt a childlike approach to our thought processes, our curiosity will increase, and therefore so will our creativity. Children are more open to exploring the unfamiliar. It's about allowing ourselves the freedom to explore the unknown and challenge accepted thinking and practice.

It's also about broadening and expanding our interests. We expand our vocabulary through reading books. We discover new passions and hidden talents through trying new things, talking to different people and reframing how we approach things.

We choose to maintain space for the imagination beyond the normal and routine. Weekends may require us to complete our usual chores, but we still have time to improvise a new culinary masterpiece, develop an idea for a new hobby, or jot down our thoughts for a story, a book or a piece of music.

It's about associating with others to talk about new ideas, to learn from others you see as having a particular passion or expertise, and to imagine how to take this further. Creative coach Dan Goodwin encourages us to develop a 'Curiosity Habit' so we stay constantly inquisitive about our world and how things (and people) operate. Isaac Newton once said, 'If I have been able to see further than others, it is because I stood on the shoulders of giants'.

For the organisation: igniting the creativity spark

A workplace culture that encourages staff to speak up and share their ideas provides a brain-safe environment that fosters imagination and creativity.

Beyond just listening, it's important that we channel ideas towards a pathway where they can be discussed and explored. This might mean establishing an ideas tank, from which individual and team members along with managers can choose ideas for further deliberation and/or implementation.

Those ideas not selected for action still need to be investigated and constructive feedback provided on how they could be pitched differently or improved on. Demonstrating a genuine appreciation of *all* ideas fosters a continuing creative spark.

Collaboration
Side by side

It's the late 1950s. You're a teenage boy called John living with your aunt, and all you want in life is to play the guitar and listen to rock 'n' roll. A couple of things are probably going to happen: first, you are probably going to drive said aunt off her rocker; and second, you are going to have to form a band, because if you're not Elvis, everyone knows you need a band to play rock 'n' roll. Besides which, you're pretty good at coming up with the start and the end of a song; you just get stuck with the middle eight bars. They're tricky. Thankfully, a mate of a mate introduces you to some bass player called Paul from across town, and together, when you sing in your aunt's bathroom (to get the sound right), you sound — well, amazing. Now if you can just come up with a name that's better than The Crickets, you'll be set. Because you love Buddy Holly. And you love a good beat, hey ...

The greatest ideas in history have rarely come from a single source. Rather, they have sprung from collaborations. 'No man is an island.' We need social interaction.

**WORKING TOGETHER HAS SHAPED
OUR EVOLUTION. LIVING IN COMMUNITIES MEANS
SHARING TASKS, DEVELOPING NEW SKILLS
COLLABORATIVELY, ACCELERATING CHANGE.
HARNESSING THE ENERGY AND THOUGHTS OF
OTHERS PRODUCES A MULTIPLIER EFFECT.**

In other words, the outcome of many brains working together is greater than the sum of their parts.

Connecting at a social level is highly motivating. Providing a safe work environment free from threat drives engagement and performance. A brain that is relaxed is more open to connecting and collaborating, to considering alternatives and contributing.

Start with connection

Collaboration is a consequence of connection.

We are social creatures. We love nothing better than to hang out with each other, whether at work, rest or play. Our success as a species is in large part due to our social intelligence and our ability to interact and relate to one another.

We are born immature, defenceless, incapable of looking after ourselves. Without the ability to bond with our parents, we simply would not have survived as a species. This is perhaps why we attribute such importance to that first smile at the age of six weeks and the intensely strong bond between child and parent.

Researchers Felix Warneken and Michael Tomasello showed that infants aged 14 to 18 months will help others to fetch out-of-reach objects or open cabinets, even though they have no expectation of reward or praise. Cultivating such selfless support promotes social group bonding. You scratch my back and I'll scratch yours.

Matt Lieberman, a social cognitive neuroscientist at UCLA, describes social intelligence as the fourth element critical to our survival, after food, water and shelter. This makes sense, because while selfish behaviour is important for short-term self-preservation, cooperation is the better strategy for building the community, mutual understanding and tolerance of difference that we need as social beings.

The social brain hypothesis, which has been around since the 1980s, suggests that one of the reasons humans developed such a large forebrain was to manage the complexity of our social systems when we started to live in groups and incorporate verbal language.

Anthropologist Robin Dunbar (1998) suggested the size of the brain determined the size of our social groups. *Dunbar's number* refers to the maximum number of individual stable social relationships we form, which he puts at around 150. Of these, about 100 are casual friends and the other 50 are our more intimate friends whom we see on a regular basis. We might have 15 really good friends, those we are happy to discuss most things with, and finally we have around five 'BFFs'. In comparison, the great apes, with their smaller brains, maintain social groups of up to a maximum of 80.

Of course with the advent of social media, the question asked now is, are our Facebook friends or Twitter followers part of that group? These social media outlets have broadened our networks so many more people may have heard of us, but our level of interaction, depending on the amount of time invested, limits our capacity to build quality interactions. In Dunbar's view, 'the amount of social capital we have is pretty fixed. It involves time investment. If we garner connections with more people, we distribute our fixed amount of social capital more thinly so the average capital per person is lower'.

Ask any teacher and they will know the difference between getting to know and understand a class of 15 students compared with a class of 40. A team manager looking after 20 staff will have a very different grasp of the group dynamics than will a manager of a team of 150.

Our previous thinking about human evolution was that early man formed groups to be more effective as hunters. This view is now being challenged by the likes of anthropologist Robert Sussman, author of *Man the Hunted*, who suggests that early hominids were small in stature, ate fruit and nuts and were more likely to be prey than predator. His view is that we developed collaborative skills to stay safe.

SURVIVAL, THEN, IS ABOUT HAVING THE SOCIAL SMARTS TO STAY SAFE THROUGH COOPERATION AND KEEPING YOUR WITS ABOUT YOU.

Watch any sci-fi movie about future world domination by robots or zombies, and the plot will reveal how a small band of heroes cleverly overcomes the odds to avoid being hunted down and eliminated. We are the hunted rather than the hunter. Of course, the story will include a romantic interest because how else will our clever band of collaborators perpetuate their smarts?

IN PEACE AND WAR, RELATIONSHIPS MATTER

Making connections. That's what we are good at. We make connections with each other through our relationships, and we make connections or associations between what we face now and our past experiences. Both types of connection rely on our brain.

We like best those people we see as similar to ourselves and connect with them more readily. Familiarity breeds connection.

It's important to have and maintain exceptional social skills because relationships are important at every level. At work, when we don't feel part of a tribe, our lack of relatedness manifests in poorer performance, lower engagement and higher staff turnover. Why stay in a place you don't feel part of or where you don't feel valued?

Social exclusion, whether intentional or through apathy, causes social pain, which lowers self-esteem, confidence and mood (see figure 11.1).

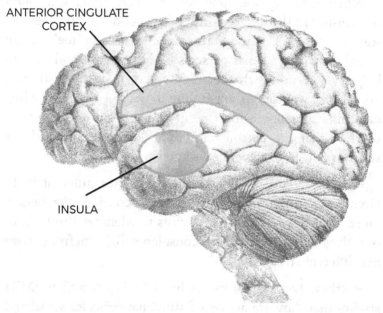

Figure 11.1: social pain hurts

A study in 2003 by Matthew Lieberman and Naomi Eisenberger used the computer game Cyberball to show how the social pain of exclusion (in this case a participant is deliberately excluded from the game) activates two brain areas, the anterior cingulate cortex (ACC) and the insula. These are the same two areas involved in registering physical pain.

Social pain hurts just as much as physical pain, and yet we often overlook its significance or downplay it. While we might rush to the hospital if a friend has broken their leg, we might suggest that another friend pull themselves together if they are getting over a relationship breakup.

We use the language of physical pain when describing how our heart has been broken or how someone hurt our feelings. In times of trouble, to relieve the pain caused by a social snub we seek solace in the company of others.

When meeting someone for the first time, our brain determines in the first one-fifth of a second whether they are friend or foe. While the brain's default is set to 'foe', we use visual cues of the other person's body language and tone to help us determine whether they could, in fact, be 'friend'. Sometimes we use our gut feeling to decide whether we like or dislike someone, which might be based on no more than the fact that the person reminds us, either consciously or subconsciously, of someone we know.

What is interesting is how the brain uses different brain circuits when determining this. If we consider the person more like us, we use similar circuits to when we think about ourselves. When the person is considered different from us, we use different circuits.

Matthew Lieberman, in his book *Social*, describes fMRI studies that show we use two distinct networks for social and non-social thinking. When we stop using one network, we automatically slip into the other. Lieberman proposes that this gets us ready to interact socially within our world and is why we are hardwired to connect.

The birds and the bees do it, and so do we. Cooperate, that is.

Far from being a unique human trait, examples of cooperative behaviours in different species are to be found everywhere. You will never see an ant stuck in a traffic jam or a bee lost without its dancing shoes. Flocks of birds, shoals of fish — many creatures use mass cooperation for herd protection and mutual benefit.

Physicist and author Fritjof Capra observes, 'Nature nurtures life through communities. Life that started over 3 billion years ago took over the planet through networking not combat'.

But even knowing we have nature on our side, collaboration isn't always easy. Sometimes we seem determined to stuff things up. How often do you hear of previously good relationships turning sour, of complaints not listened to, of unequal effort applied to shared tasks?

'When I die, I want the people I did group projects with to lower me into my grave, so they can let me down one last time.'

Anonymous

When negotiations or collaborative efforts break down, the reasons often cited relate to miscommunication or misunderstanding by one or both parties. Despite all our cleverness and ability to innovate, create and design, we are sometimes really bad at attending to the basic premise of our social intelligence. Which is a pity, because if we took the time to relate, to listen, to understand, it could in many instances lead to a different outcome.

Thankfully the rapid advancement of understanding in the area of social cognition provides us with a new blueprint to better navigate the tricky environment of other people's minds, needs, desires and agendas. We truly are together alone. The primal drive for self-preservation keeps us selfish. We end up with the paradox of duality: the need to look after number one while being part of a social network.

PLEASE DON'T DISCONNECT ME

Joining in isn't always easy, especially joining a pre-existing social network. Think of the new kid at school who must negotiate a way to be included in new friendship groups. It can be an isolating and difficult time, especially if current group members see the newcomer as 'different'. Fitting in may involve adopting the same dress code, hairstyle or way of speaking. How often have you looked back at old photos from a different era and thought, 'What was I thinking!'? We bought into flared jeans, wide ties and big hair not because it suited us but because it confirmed we were part of a group.

Attending a conference, a networking event or even a social gathering where you don't know anyone can be challenging, especially if you have an introverted nature. That's why we often choose to hook up with someone we know, even if the connection is tenuous.

We seek commonality. The most common question people meeting for the first time will ask each other is, 'And what is it you do?' This provides an opportunity to look for shared interests, views and background, and is certainly more interesting than talking about the weather (although even that topic is better than not sharing any conversation at all).

In certain types of jobs social interaction and collaboration are essential. However, it's still important to allow people the choice to think through a problem or come up with a new idea on their own. Forcing people to work collaboratively all the time 'because that's the way we work here' doesn't necessarily suit all tasks at all times. Some brains need more quiet time alone to come up with their greatest insights.

The role of a manager or leader includes ensuring that a person who is naturally introverted, shy or socially anxious is not made to feel isolated.

Social psychologist John Cacioppo has studied the biological effects of loneliness. Social isolation, whether through choice or circumstance, impacts our health and cognition. A lonely person's brain is on permanent guard duty, hyper-alert to threat from the outside world. When we feel lonely, our levels of stress hormones, including cortisol, are elevated, our sleep is disturbed and any negative experience of events magnified.

Our health and cognition depends on our social brain.

While undertaking my nursing training at St Thomas' Hospital in London I spent some time living in a rented room at the top of a house, separated from the family below. Though I had people around me and worked every day with others, I was lonely. I made the decision to move to a shared flat because I realised the negative impact my hermit-like existence was having on my health and wellbeing.

What I hadn't appreciated was how loneliness reduces our cognitive skills, or I might have moved sooner! Social studies have shown how the greater the *perceived* social isolation, the poorer our cognitive performance, with cognitive decline in every domain except working memory and episodic performance.

Many modern workplaces make an effort to ensure new employees are taken care of, providing a buddy system or having a manager check up on how a newbie is fitting in and becoming 'one of the tribe'. Group social activities and water-cooler chats are all about breaking the ice and getting more 'like' one another. That's great for the newbies, but what about those who have been around for a while? Does your workplace have a system to check in to see that everyone feels included, whether they have been there for five minutes, five weeks or five years?

BEING PART OF THE IN-CROWD

To be part of a collaborative group you must first be accepted.

If your first impression of a person is that they are 'like' you and therefore one of the 'in' group, you are more likely to trust them, which makes sense. Think about the time you were asked to work with someone you didn't like. Chances are you didn't produce your best work, because your focus was on protecting yourself and watching your back.

Breaking down the barriers – a shared bond

Wendy had been working in her company for over three years and was anticipating a promotion, so felt a little wary when Belinda was invited to join the team project that Wendy had been leading for the previous six months. Initial conversations between the two women felt stifled and awkward. Wendy feared being usurped by Belinda, whom she saw as a rival for the coveted promotion. Belinda tried hard to get Wendy to accept her but sensed Wendy didn't like her. Following a particularly terse conversation in a team meeting, their manager spoke to each of them separately. He desperately wanted to reduce the animosity that looked ready to break out into open warfare. His concern was that the lack of group cohesion was threatening to undermine the whole team's performance.

The following week, the manager was amazed to walk past Wendy and Belinda in fits of laughter as they shared a private joke.

Belinda, who was new to the area, had just enrolled her youngest child at the same soccer club that Wendy's son already belonged to. The common bond of children with similar interests was all it took to break down the social barriers and allow them to form a common 'in group'.

We form 'in groups' all the time. Television producers use this to their advantage, getting us to watch numerous reality shows because we like to watch and associate with people like us. We can relate to people like us as they pursue a dream of becoming a pop star, chef or lucky winner of a new home. Game shows design their live studio audiences to be just like us so watching the excitement of the studio audience excites us too.

LET'S GET PHYSICAL

The Inuit greet each other by rubbing noses. (Why risk frostbite by taking off your gloves when your nose is already exposed?) The Brits love to shake hands. Europeans kiss cheeks, twice in France, thrice in Switzerland. You might get a hug in the States or a bow in Japan.

When we greet each other through some form of physical contact the brain is triggered to release oxytocin, the so-called trust hormone. No wonder doctors have used that immortal line, 'Trust me, I'm a doctor'. It's not just their expertise or authority that counts, but the physicality of the laying on of hands during an examination as well.

Oxytocin has been shown to be important in other aspects of our social lives, including:

» increasing our social skills and reducing social anxieties and shyness

» increasing our self-esteem and levels of optimism

» reducing cortisol levels and lowering our blood pressure

» increasing our generosity

» making us happier.

How does this show up? Imagine you have just spent time in a meeting with someone you like and trust. If, on your way back to your car, you are approached by a stranger raising money for charity, you are more likely to stop and donate a more generous amount than you might have done otherwise.

When we feel happier, we are more collaborative and cooperative, and boosting happiness comes from human connection. Paul Zak has found that eight hugs a day is all it takes. If you are hug averse, a gentle touch on another person's arm works, as does having a massage or snuggling up on the couch with your partner.

Zak believes that while oxytocin plays a vital role in boosting empathy, generosity and trust, thus 'wiring' us to connect, business and economics ignore the biological foundations of reciprocity — because we are risk-averse. Think of how a board of executives or senior managers, when looking at whether to share information and knowledge with another organisation, will first consider all the potential risks, rather than looking at how such reciprocity could boost future business growth and opportunities.

A major stumbling block for change initiatives and collaboration is our perception that the potential risk outweighs any upside. And because the pain associated with this downside is always greater than any reward, the brain takes a lot of convincing to think otherwise.

Managers and leaders who are aware of this can help by using social interaction to mitigate the stress response. In a world increasingly dominated by anxiety and depression, socialisation is becoming an ever more important management tool to build that sense of tribe, belonging and contribution.

Creating a collaborative culture

Beyond individual contribution to a group, cultivating a work culture based on trust and collaboration, as Janine Garner writes in her book *From Me to We*, provides opportunity for businesses:

» Step out of the danger zone of the status quo. Commercial collaboration is all about embracing change, promoting growth and possibility.

» Build a network that pushes boundaries and stretches thinking. We experience our greatest reward when feeling that little bit of stretch, the mental challenge to step up and do that bit extra. Getting a little shove from a supportive network keeps us accountable and encourages us to contribute more.

Zappos, the global online shoe company, has built a culture based on collaboration and contribution. One of its programs encourages staff to reward a coworker who has been observed to go above and beyond the call of regular customer service or work obligation.

This has proven to be a highly successful initiative because it is founded on the basis of mutual trust and collaboration. It elevates community levels of oxytocin and drives the collaborative spirit. At a societal level this is reflected in lower levels of crime and better economic conditions.

In 2013 The Reputation Institute, a global private consulting firm, released its fourth annual list of 50 countries ranked by trust, admiration, respect and affinity. The top five were Canada, Sweden, Switzerland, Australia and Norway. To see where your country sits in this ranking, simply go to www. reputationinstitute.com. Country and profession aside, we can all use our social brain awareness to actively participate in building a collaborative work culture.

ENVIRONMENTAL ENGINEERING

Collaboration is enhanced by the right environment. Working together needs space. The way your working space is designed can have a huge impact on your productivity, level of innovation and collaboration.

Steve Jobs was an early innovator in this area. He devised the Pixar offices so that people would be forced to bump into each other during their working day. Why? Because of the value of water-cooler chats, bathroom chats and lunch break chats for increasing productivity and collaboration. Now if you're thinking, 'Weren't we told earlier that working without interruptions is better for productivity?', that's absolutely correct. Except it isn't about working consistently from dawn to dusk, it's about organising focused time into manageable chunks.

Once, offices were devised to allow several people to share a local environment. Then it was decided that to accommodate larger numbers of people working together, it was better to put people either in cubicles or in open-plan offices. The pros and cons of these are well established. Yes, we are social creatures and benefit from sharing a work area with other people, but the cubicles themselves are soulless. Not only that, but the forced semi-isolation means while you have less visual contact with your work buddy next door, you must still deal with all the audible distractions of their phone calls, conversations and tapping keyboard.

Now the trend is towards activity-based workplaces. No longer chained to a desk or hot-desking, employees are encouraged to work collaboratively with others on their shared projects, which will require them to have meetings or one-on-one time, as required.

Google, always an innovative place to work, embraced the opportunity to do something different. The first activity-based workplace (ABW) in Sydney garnered much praise. Instead of a personal space with a desk, employees were provided with only a small locker in which to store personal items and work equipment such as laptops. They had no designated workspace. Instead, people chose to work in the area and with the people most relevant to their particular project.

When I visited a pilot ABW in Perth being trialled by BankWest in 2012, it felt slightly surreal walking into an open space with brightly coloured orange walls, textured surfaces and unusual-looking chairs with what looked like giant rabbit ears — features that would not be out of place in a modern art gallery. With no 'C suite' of offices, all the executives worked alongside other staff members.

In an age of increasing equality, having the CEO working alongside you, visible and accessible, might make you feel good. But, like being made to sit next to the teacher in a classroom, it can also induce a stress response!

Activity-based workplaces have their advocates and detractors. It's been reported that changes to our working environment can cause increased stress to the detriment of relationships *outside work*. High stress reduces prefrontal control of emotions, leading to greater emotional volatility and irritability. If you are feeling snappy or crabby at work, it's all too easy to take that bad mood home.

JOINING THE HUB

Collaborative workspaces for unrelated businesses have become enormously popular around the world over the past few years. Melbourne, Sydney, Amsterdam and Bristol all have their Hubs. There is CitizenSpace in San Francisco, Workspace in Vancouver, Whitespace in London, Gravity in Sydney, the Hive in Hong Kong and SpaceCubed in Perth. The concept is that for a modest joining fee you can access the common facilities provided.

On my first visit to the Melbourne Hub, I was immediately struck by the energy and vitality of the people working there. It was a hive of activity, literally buzzing with the thoughts and computers of those at work.

For solopreneurs and small enterprises of two or three people, these spaces work brilliantly in providing opportunities to 'bump into' others. This induces a sense of collaboration, camaraderie and belonging that moves the brain into a 'towards' state that is ideal for good thinking.

Team intelligence

'Michael I've already told you, if you want to play with Jack, you have to share your toys!'

For a four-year-old, learning to share a plaything doesn't always come easily. It can be a painful lesson for all involved, but it is an essential social skill that enables us as adults to know the social etiquette required to build and maintain relationships, share ideas and work together on projects.

But not everyone wants to play nice. Egos, temper tantrums and hissy fits make frequent appearances on the work stage. As Casey Stengel said, 'Getting good players is easy — getting them to play together is the hard part'. Pity the poor manager trying desperately to get their team members to *talk* to each other, let alone work collaboratively on the project at hand. No wonder the task is sometimes compared to herding cats.

Team intelligence (or collective intelligence, as it is sometimes called) can be a big ask — give me a bunch of four-year-olds any day. But the brain science can help us understand what works to develop effective teams. Trust plays a vital role. How many times have you been on a team-building course where you have to play the game of falling backwards, hoping (praying!) that your partner in the exercise will catch you?

While it's nice to know your work colleagues care enough about you to prevent you from hurting yourself, at least in a workshop environment, does this actually translate into anything useful in the workplace itself?

Teaming people up doesn't mean they necessarily want to or will work together, or that anything meaningful will result from the collaboration. Every brain is different. We have different levels of general and emotional intelligence, different agendas, different opinions, different ways of doing things. So it's not about just sticking the brainiest bunch of people together.

PLAY THE GAME

Motivation design strategist Jason Fox talks about how to motivate people in the workplace using gamification principles. He works with companies to help them remove those points of friction in the workplace that hold us back in how well we work. From the brain's point of view, when we feel rewarded by our sense of progress, we release greater amounts of dopamine. More dopamine primes our brain to continue with the activity it finds so rewarding.

Gamification is attracting a lot of interest in the business world as a means to assist in re-engaging a disengaged workforce. The principle behind it is not about just playing games and having fun, but about understanding the drivers that really motivate us to do something. Watch children at play and it will be immediately obvious how completely focused and absorbed they are in their activity, lost in the moment and the joy of the game.

FINDING THE 'C' FACTOR

The collective intelligence of a group has been found to be more predictive overall than the IQ of individual members.

Collective thinking and behaviour, as with that of individuals, can be smart or downright dumb. What matters is finding the right behavioural traits that will contribute to collective success. Configuring a team that is consistently capable of producing good ideas and solving problems is what matters.

Thomas Malone, Director of the MIT Centre for Collective Intelligence and author of *The Future of Work*, defines intelligence at an individual level as being good at picking up new things quickly, whereas group intelligence implies being able to perform well on a wide range of tasks.

Anita Woolley and others from MIT, Carnegie Mellon and Union universities have shown that the 'C' factor, or collective intelligence, of a group correlates strongly with:

» the degree of social sensitivity in the group

» the ability to take turns in speaking

» the number of women in the group.

The eyes have it — social sensitivity

Anita Woolley's work confirms that our ability to read people's emotions by looking them in the eye is linked to our social intelligence and performance in team-based problem solving. In today's and tomorrow's workplace, developing our social sensitivity is an essential skill that should be on every organisation's agenda. It's about boosting performance by developing a work culture that is sensitive to the needs of all its staff.

The fact that social media and communication rely less and less on direct, face-to-face contact is a cause for concern that needs to be addressed now.

Taking turns does matter

Some people do like the sound of their own voice, but if one group member is allowed to dominate, team intelligence is restricted: the quieter voices fail to get heard and the group risks missing out on some really good ideas! It's more than just being polite. Ensuring that everyone is encouraged to add their voice to the conversation and share opinions is a social skill we can all benefit from. An essential skill of all great leaders is the practice of speaking less and listening more.

Girl power

It was Jim Carrey who shared the immortal line, 'Behind every great man there is a woman rolling her eyes'.

Yes, gender does play a role here, but it's important to interpret the data correctly. Including women in a team statistically increases collective intelligence, because women tend to have higher levels of social sensitivity.

How many women should each team have? There isn't a definitive answer! It's not a case of just being seen to be politically correct. Woolley's research suggests that recruiting members to a team based on their level of social sensitivity will naturally lead to the inclusion of more women.

SMELLS LIKE TEAM SPIRIT

It is the collective power of many heads working together that produces the biggest impact on the quality and quantity of work produced.

In his book *The Wisdom of Crowds*, James Surowiecki illustrates how crowd wisdom can benefit collective problem solving, coordination and cooperation, and how adding diversity to the mix leads to greater independence and decentralisation of thought. In other words, just like our Goldilocks brain, crowds need to reflect a delicate balance between size and mix.

That's why when it works well, team intelligence flows like water. When called to a medical emergency, the 'crash call' team swings into action, each person understanding their role and function, working alongside their team members, anticipating and responding to the crisis as it unfolds before them. Even in a crowd, there will be a director or conductor everyone looks to for guidance and reassurance.

THE PROBLEM WITH GROUPTHINK

Handled well, teamwork can be fun, challenging and immensely rewarding. Done badly, and it may end up a frustrating, exhausting and demoralising experience.

Teamwork induces so much difficulty because people are different; our brains are wired differently so we perceive things differently. Emotions, being infectious, play a big role in team effectiveness. It only takes one person to be very negative or very positive, and the rest of the team will follow suit in a storm of emotional contagion.

'Groupthink', writes Irving Janis, 'occurs when a group makes bad decisions because group pressure leads to a deterioration in mental efficiency and moral judgment'. What behaviours promote groupthink? Perhaps surprisingly, what are otherwise perceived as positive traits can lead us into the perilous waters of groupthink:

» It can be immensely rewarding to be included in a group. Being awarded group status elevates how we feel about our situation and is associated with dopamine release. The promise of more dopamine drives our inclination to stay group oriented.

» We like and relate to other group members. Getting along with your colleagues is a great way to ensure you work more effectively together. Liking others and being liked contribute to the 'feel good' factor.

» The group defines itself as separate or apart from others. This makes it all the more special as an experience. You are removing yourself from the influence of others outside the group.

» In many groups, the nominated leader is seen as the most powerful or influential member. Continuing membership of the group may require the leader's ongoing support so staying on-side with the group, and especially the leader, matters.

Sometimes our desire to be part of a group doesn't turn out the way we'd hoped. If that happens, we face a difficult choice. We can choose to stay and accept we may not achieve our desired outcome, or we can choose to leave and live with the social pain of exclusion.

One of the classic examples of the failure of groupthink centres on JFK and the Bay of Pigs fiasco of 1961. Kennedy had relied on an inner circle of trusted advisers to determine what to do about Fidel Castro, the Cuban leader perceived by the Americans as a threat. They wanted to get rid of him, and the CIA devised a plan using Cuban exiles to invade the island and overthrow the Cuban revolution. It all went horribly wrong and resulted in the surrender of 1200 of the 1400-strong invasion force and a number of deaths. Contributing factors later identified included:

» *a lack of dissenters willing to speak up.* Group cohesion is a nice, comfortable space, but if no one is willing to stand up and question group thinking or decisions, wrong decisions will go unchallenged.

» *the illusion of unanimity.* If group members fail to voice their private dissenting opinion, they discourage others in the group who may be thinking the same thing from speaking out.

» *employing deliberate tactics to isolate known dissenters*

» *playing down or ignoring risk.* No one likes to think their ideas could fail. It's like some of the investment prospectuses of the nineties that promised investors huge returns. The possibility of an economic downturn was never considered, because house and commodity prices would always increase in value, wouldn't they?

» *overconfidence.* Experience can be a tough teacher. While self-belief is good, being overconfident or dismissive of another person's strengths and ability can result in a hard lesson of defeat. Notions of invincibility are best reserved for superheroes. Recognising where our kryptonite lies helps us to recognise our own fallibility and accept we will not always be right.

Team work

Countless ideas can contribute to team performance improvement. The following is therefore not an exhaustive list.

1. Select team members carefully.
   » Recognise each individual's qualities and strengths and give them the autonomy to work independently within the group. This is about recognising we each have different preferred ways of operating, and best performance occurs when we are granted that flexibility.
   » Identify the social sensitivity level of an individual. How well are they likely to interact with others? How attuned are they to recognising and aligning with group dynamics?
   » Include gender diversity. (Women and men work really well together.)
2. Set the ground rules for the team.
   » All team members are encouraged to be accessible to one another to make data sharing and support easier.
   » All team members should share a clear vision of what the team is attempting to achieve and be able to articulate it.

> » Each team member is expected to act in a fully transparent way with no hidden agenda.

> » Each team member must feel safe to share ideas and ask clarifying questions.

> » There is a general consensus around the common shared values.

> » The team has a specified leader or manager who promotes open communication, encourages interaction and rewards collaboration.

3. Review the team's work.

> » We feel motivated by our sense of progress. Regular check-ins and appropriate celebration of progress markers along the way ensure productivity is recognised.

The 2008 Gensler Workplace Survey showed that those working in top-performing companies had a 50 per cent greater satisfaction level than those in average-performing companies.

What that means is that high-performance workplaces have worked out that staff who are engaged and motivated to do the work they do are happier, stay in their position longer, and are more contributive, cooperative and productive. In a subsequent survey, Gensler identified a three-point formula for organisational success.

1. workplace design prioritising collaboration

2. doing meaningful work where individuals get a sense of making a difference at the personal and organisational level, and

3. nurturing the development of great interpersonal working relationships.

In other words, facilitating individual focus when needed and providing for collaborative work. Their culture is one of collaboration, and that drives performance and profits.

KEY 12
Leadership
Thought before action

'If you want to build a ship, don't drum up the men to gather wood, divide the work, and give orders. Instead, teach them to yearn for the vast and endless sea.'
Antoine de Saint-Exupéry

We seem to be obsessed with leadership. Leadership programs abound, and if you have a few spare minutes to catch up on some reading, as of April 2015 Amazon.com listed 132 976 books on the subject, up from 107 326 when I looked at about the same time in 2014.

What is leadership? It is something we observe in others and sometimes in ourselves. We find security in following the vision of a leader who we perceive has our best interests at heart.

Leadership programs have traditionally focused on goal directives, technology and expertise. But the new, emerging leadership is people focused, because it is people who drive business performance and success through common values, beliefs and desires. Self-directed leadership is about understanding what motivates and drives us. It provides meaning for what we do, so we can focus on what is required and get on with it. As Ken Blanchard says, 'Real leadership happens when you are not there'.

'What makes a good leader?' is the question most frequently asked, along with 'What do we need to ensure leaders develop the skillsets needed to provide effective leadership?'

Findings from social cognitive neuroscience can help answer these questions by showing the *what*, and the *how* appropriate to the modern workplace.

What makes a good leader?

What has neuroscience shown us about leadership?

» We can use the understanding of our brain's natural plasticity to create those habits and thinking patterns that boost emotional intelligence and foster an open mindset.

» We can foster our social intelligence to gain a greater understanding of others who may have a different perspective or viewpoint.

» We can ensure that our brain is as fit and healthy as possible by adopting a healthy lifestyle so we are mentally prepared to make important decisions and solve problems quickly and easily.

In other words, exceptional leaders can be created through incorporating understandings from the brain science that help us develop a brain that is fit, flexible and agile.

A number of desirable characteristics are talked about as prerequisites for good leadership. Which ones do *you* value most?

Start by listing the five leaders you most admire and then determine what leadership characteristics or values they hold in common. These might include being a good listener, an effective communicator, a person of high integrity and trust, or a good role model.

Then ask yourself the following questions:

1. Do these apply to me and/or the person I currently work for?

2. Which values or characteristics do I want to be recognised for?

3. Should leaders be recognised for their technical ability and results, or their social skills?

Yes, number three is a trick question, because the answer is preferably both.

Matt Lieberman, in his book *Social*, describes the findings of a survey undertaken by David Rock from the Neuroleadership Institute and Management Research Group that reveals fewer than 1 per cent of leaders were rated as being high on goal focus *and* social skills. Rock builds on previous work by leadership experts Zenger and Folkman, who showed how that 1 per cent will be perceived as great leaders by 72 per cent of their employees, compared with 14 per cent for results (goal) focused leaders and 12 per cent for social focused leaders.

Great leaders develop the capacity to alternate rapidly between analytical and social thought.

Because leadership can be learned, the solution is to provide a program that enhances capability in both thinking patterns. In addition, because we live in such a fast-paced world, being able to demonstrate this agility fast is paramount to leadership effectiveness in the modern workplace.

Laying a foundation for the future

Anyone in a position of leadership knows their tenure is limited. What matters is to develop an appropriate succession plan by recognising the potential in those who will follow, mentoring and guiding them, and knowing when the time has come for them to step up to their new position.

It's like being a parent. We look after our children, nurture them, keep them healthy and propel them towards adulthood. Great parenting is about making yourself redundant, so when your child leaves home or starts their first job, they are prepared to move into the big wide world. Your job is done.

Of course, neither parenting nor leadership is always easy, and one of the hardest things is knowing when the right time to let go is. When our son was about five, we bought him his first bicycle. It was bright red and he delighted in learning to ride. At first this took a lot of encouragement and support, and he relied heavily on his training wheels. After a little while, the time came to take the training wheels off and let him ride on his own. We were all a little apprehensive, but with one helpful shove, he was off, peddling furiously, proud as punch, and he didn't look back.

AVOIDING THE SEAGULLS

Good leaders know that by encouraging others to develop new skills and areas of expertise for themselves, those people too will reach the time when their training wheels can come off, when they can step up. Unfortunately, not all leaders have this skillset. Some feel threatened by the prospect of being displaced and adopt a defensive approach that may not always be to the benefit of those they serve.

Dr Bob Nelson, who works in the area of motivation and management, describes the type of leader or manager who abdicates this responsibility as a 'seagull'.

Loud, aggressive birds, seagulls swoop in periodically, make a big noise, stir everyone up and then fly off, often leaving a big pile of you-know-what behind. Seagull managers and leaders are a menace because they deprive their staff of the opportunity to develop their potential. They also deprive the organisation of the next generation of potential leaders.

This is all about status. Some choose to demonstrate their status by reminding people who they are and making a lot of noise. Some, if they see themselves as beleaguered and needing to fend off status threat, may choose to respond in a threatening or belligerent manner.

BRINGING OUT THE BEST IN OTHERS

Leaders and mentors often know intuitively how to bring out the best in other people. They can of course also learn and develop these skills using what is understood from the social cognitive neuroscience.

There are five strategies that can be employed here.

Listen

In our fragmented and highly distracting world, giving another person our complete and undivided attention has become a challenge. We are all so busy thinking about what we want to add to a conversation that we stop listening to what is actually being said. Practising stepping back, inviting someone to speak out fully without interruption or judgement, has two major benefits. First, the person delivering the message feels fully heard, which is very empowering. Second, the receiver actually hears the whole message without the usual filters, which deepens their understanding.

Great leaders listen more and speak less.

Speak

Choice of language has an enormous impact on how a message is received. Choosing our words carefully, thinking before we speak, is essential to avoid the classic 'foot in mouth' syndrome. We have all probably made those horrible gaffes: like asking a woman when her baby is due, when she's just put on a little weight; or saying something dreadfully insensitive, like the former BP CEO Tony Hayward who in the aftermath of the deadly 2010 Gulf of Mexico oil spill complained, 'There's no one who wants this over more than I do. I would like my life back'. Ouch.

Reflect

Busy CEOs and leaders need the time to pause and reflect, to think about their thinking. This metacognition allows us to consider and compare, to promote dialogue and broaden perspective. In our busy daily lives, time for reflection promotes responsive rather than reactive thought.

Inquire

Staying curious is not just good for creativity and collaboration; it opens up new possibilities through the insights gained and promotes change in our thinking and our behaviour.

Connect

As any salesperson will advise, connection is all about the follow-up, which deepens and gives more meaning to our relationships. Great leaders understand they have to be seen and heard to establish trust, relatedness and empathy. They manifest their credentials for leadership by demonstrating through their behaviour that they are leaders worth following. The payoff here, as revealed by the University of Warwick, is that the leader who cares and fully commits to investing in their employees health and wellbeing will be rewarded by an increase in discretionary effort and up to 12 per cent higher productivity. It's good for the individual and for the bottom line.

The ones in the wings

We tend to think of a leader as the head of an organisation, such as the CEO or business owner, but in reality an organisation or business will have many leaders. They may not be on the payroll for their leadership, but their behaviour and attitude defines them as such. These are the people who spot a potential problem and head it off before it can build from a summer storm to a Category 5 cyclone. They are the ones who notice that a coworker's performance or behaviour is a little off and check in to ask if everything is okay.

Leaders see the need for things to get done.

My friend and colleague Graeme Cowan is a leader in building resilience, mental wellbeing and performance. His own experience of severe depression while a senior executive transformed his attitude to how companies deal with adversity. A large part of his work today is in promoting the RUOK concept. This is critical work because the incidence of mental illness — depression, anxiety and psychosis — is escalating in our society. Depression is now the second leading cause of workplace disability worldwide.

Gavin Larkin started RUOK Day in 2009 following the suicide of his father. The event, held each September, is a reminder for us to check in with others and ask, 'How are you doing?' because the reality is we often choose to ignore or fail to recognise the warning signs. Starting a conversation can make the difference, because human connection gives hope. The statistics tell us that talking to someone experiencing suicidal ideation about how they feel will significantly reduce the chance of their taking that final step.

Naturally, good leaders at any level don't wait for RUOK Day; they look out for their people every day.

As Peter Baines, who started the charity Hands Across the Water, says, 'It's what people do, not the position they hold, that makes the real difference'.

We are human beings who connect, and we demonstrate our understanding of each other through our interpersonal interactions. Leadership is all about acting with humanity, because at the end of the day that's what counts.

ONCE MORE, WITH MEANING

Feeling engaged with the task before us, and being motivated to do it well, is what gives meaning and purpose to what we do. It comes from our sense of 'belonging'.

One of the worst jobs I ever had was in data entry. My daily task was to sit in front of a computer, sifting through files, picking out the appropriate details, coding them and entering them into a database. It was mind-blowingly boring. After a couple of weeks I was ready to commit hara-kiri or pull my toenails out one by one rather than face yet more tedious hours glued to the computer screen and that never-ending stack of files.

Why was it so awful? Because I ascribed little value to the work I was doing.

I consider myself incredibly blessed that over the course of my working career I have for the vast majority of time found myself doing work I absolutely love. This has to be a good thing, because we spend an extraordinary amount of our life as adults working to earn a salary that pays the bills, feeds the kids and keeps a roof over our heads. I recognise too that for some of us there isn't always a choice in the work we do. We can be in a job we loathe with people we dislike, but have to do it because there simply is no option B.

Identifying what it is that keeps us motivated is derived from the perspective we take. This is illustrated perfectly by the story of the three stonemasons.

A man saw three stonemasons working together busily and asked each in turn what he was doing. The first stonemason replied, 'I turn big rocks into smaller rocks'. He was task

orientated. The second stonemason said, 'I am feeding my family'. He was career orientated. The third stonemason said, 'I am building a cathedral'. He was working to a calling.

Perspective of purpose provides us with the *why* behind what we do, and it's not necessarily about the money. When we are working to our strengths and enjoying a strong sense of job satisfaction, we feel more fulfilled and this can lead to:

» greater commitment to our employer or organisation

» less inclination to leave our position or job

» fewer days absent or sick

» a greater willingness to work discretionary hours (that is, without pay)

» more faith or trust in management

» more initiative

» greater team effectiveness.

I have heard Generation Ys and Millennials criticised for their unwillingness to put in the hard yards and their inflated sense of entitlement. That has not been my observation, by the way! The vast majority of the Gen Ys and Millennials I have met are highly engaged, passionate and hardworking. They demonstrate a high level of social awareness too.

This is also what the iOpener Institute found in a study that revealed Gen Ys are drawn to do work that has a strong economic or social purpose. They are not primarily motivated by incremental pay rises (though happy to accept them, if offered!).

In other words, job fulfilment wins hands down over financial reward. And this has been shown to be true cross-generationally.

Our work doesn't have to be highbrow, Nobel Prize–winning or especially different for us as individuals to find meaning. How many people do you know who may not have the best job in the world but nonetheless love it and are passionate about their role? This can include what others might consider dismissively as menial work.

In the TV program *Undercover Boss*, a CEO or manager masquerades as a new recruit in the company. The purpose is to discover not only what some of the staff think about their job, but how they interact with colleagues and what keeps them working in what could appear to be demanding, difficult or unpleasant work.

What makes the program so interesting is the genuine pride so many of these workers take in their work. This pride is what makes a workplace more efficient and productive and a happier place to work in. Their happiness is accompanied by a can-do attitude and a certainty, not just in their own ability, but of support from management if asked for.

It doesn't take much, but it's more than just knowing a staff member's name (which is a good place to start, by the way!). It's about showing a genuine interest in the person themselves through active enquiry, asking questions such as 'How is it all going?' and 'Is there anything I can help you with?'

One of the most consistent complaints I hear from employees talking about their boss or manager is, 'They know nothing about me'. Worse still is the comment, 'They never give me any positive feedback — I'm only ever told what I've done wrong.'

FEELING GOOD ABOUT OUR WORK CONTRIBUTES SIGNIFICANTLY TO OUR WELLBEING AND HAPPINESS.

If leaders genuinely want to see higher levels of engagement in their staff, it starts with helping them to see the bigger picture: tapping into the strengths and shared values to engage hearts and heads.

Organisational learning can play an important role here. Leaders and organisations can increase the value and capacity of their existing staff by reinvigorating effective learning programs to target individual career plans and performance goals.

BUILDING SELF-LEADERSHIP

The gentle art of self-directed leadership is just that; it's an imprecise art, a mental discipline of conscious choice.

We make innumerable decisions in life. Some will be good, some will be terrific and some will be plain dumb or wrong. What matters is that we direct our progress towards self-improvement and self-development. This involves change and, as we know, change can be tricky.

The status quo, as my mentor (and the founder of Thought Leaders Global) Matt Church advises, is the enemy of leadership. We have to keep moving to develop the mental flexibility and agility required to adapt and lift our game.

Checking in with our thinking starts with noticing when we are operating on autopilot. So much of our thinking as well as our behaviour is switched permanently to automatic mode, so we forget to press pause and ask, *Is this my normal mental script? Am I open to new ideas or ways of doing things? Do I think well in difficult circumstances?*

Self-awareness is the first step towards greater self-directed leadership.

It requires acknowledgement that we may not be operating in the best way, permission to be wrong and an action plan for change, with a starting date. It's about staying accountable to ourselves and others, and staying true to our own values.

There is no perfect leader, no ideal recipe for leadership. Leadership comes from a willingness to stand up and be counted, to do what you see needs doing, to be accountable for your actions and to lead others by initiating change.

It may be true that 'too many cooks spoil the broth', but creating a culture of leadership within organisations promotes business health and longevity.

It was while studying the neuroscience of leadership that I came to understand more clearly how human behaviour is based on ensuring we stay safe by minimising threat and maximising reward. By learning to recognise and act on the threats we identify in ourselves, we can develop the skillset of self-directed leadership. This can be translated into improving the quality of all our communication and interactions with others.

The TRAICE™ model

The TRAICE™ model can be used as a blueprint to help shift behaviours in a positive and enduring way. It shows us how to minimise the social pain of rejection and maximise our capacity to build strong cohesive groups.

TRAICE stands for:

Trust

Respect

Autonomy

Impartiality

Clarity

Empathy.

TRUST

When we are with someone we trust, we feel safe. The brain is in a more relaxed state and open to deeper, more meaningful conversations. We don't hold back on sharing information. We smile and interact more. We like to contribute and look out for and protect the 'trustees' in our tribe.

Trust does not develop overnight. It takes time because, as we have discussed, our default way of thinking is to assume that anything new in our environment (whether a person or a situation) presents a threat until proven otherwise.

We build trust through the behaviour we demonstrate that others observe. It requires consistency and effort on our part but is rewarded by loyalty.

We can lose trust in a moment through a careless remark or thoughtless action, and once lost it is sometimes irretrievable.

Business leaders who draw a high level of trust will enjoy a lower staff turnover (reduced costs) and an increased profit margin through greater employee contribution. Staff who feel trusted get on with their job and do it well, report higher levels of job satisfaction, take fewer days' sick leave and are happier overall. It becomes a win–win.

RESPECT

Aretha was not whistling Dixie. Respect is how we perceive our status or ranking compared with others. We might not like admitting it but we live in a hierarchical society, where everyone has a place in the pecking order of life.

Respect matters because losing it means we can no longer command control of a situation. Loss of respect diminishes our self-confidence and self-esteem. How does it make you feel when you realise your position has been challenged? Not very good, right? We can inadvertently threaten someone's rank or position through our choice of language, spoken or otherwise.

You may experience disrespect when you are not acknowledged by your boss in the morning, or you are not invited to a team meeting, or you witness an 'eye roll' when you are explaining your point of view to a colleague.

Maintaining self-respect and valuing others is the key.

AUTONOMY

Do you like being told what to do? Me neither. In fact, I've yet to meet anyone over the age of two who enjoys being directed in what they do and how they do it. Yet micromanagement is rife in many workplaces, to the detriment of the business. It stifles innovation and leads to demoralisation and disengagement.

> 'Don't tell people how to do things, tell them what to do and
> let them surprise you with their results.'
> **George S. Patton, Jr**

Having a sense that we are self-directed and have choices not only feels important to us; it affects our health and wellbeing. Providing people with choices, no matter how big or small, real or perceived, matters a great deal.

Studies have shown that the loss of autonomy associated with moving into a nursing home has a very strong link to how long a person will live.

Seeking out opportunities to enhance autonomy for ourselves and others boosts our motivation to rise to a challenge.

IMPARTIALITY

If I have $10, and after agreeing to split that money with you I give you $5, you will probably see that as fair. But what if I gave you only 50 cents? Still fair? Well I did give you something, didn't I?

Work by Tabibnia and Lieberman has shown that a perception of unfairness activates an area of the brain called the insula. Remember the last time you felt cheated by something. Remember that really bad smell your dog created? That response of unfairness (or stink) is felt as a deep visceral or gut reaction. We wrinkle up our noses in disgust!

Conversely, being treated fairly lights up the brain's reward centre, including the ventral striatum, orbitofrontal cortex (OFC), ventromedial prefrontal cortex (VMPFC) and amygdala.

Our perception of fairness is individual and unique. What you find upsetting may not faze another person. Our mental state plays an important role too. If we are already feeling a little emotional, unhappy or fragile we are more at risk of negative perceptions that can colour our interpretation of another person's intentions towards us.

A sense of fair play is critical to our physical wellbeing too. Operating in an environment where you feel unfairly criticised or micromanaged can increase your risk of coronary heart disease by 30 per cent. Unfair treatment, whether real or perceived, is a valid health consideration!

We can boost fairness by being transparent in all our interpersonal transactions. Rewarding on merit rather than social advantage would seem like a no-brainer, but the old boys' network is still alive and well in many workplaces. Favouritism can quickly sour relationships for those perceiving themselves as less favoured, leading to distrust and silo thinking.

Consistency in behaviour matters. If as a boss you are always seen to be firm but fair, your chance of successfully introducing an unpopular work policy without causing discord or resentment is much higher than if you have been seen to be inconsistent or biased or as condoning workplace bullying.

Techniques for managing unfairness include:

» reframing our perception of the incident

» choosing to look for what we can learn from the event and how to manage it differently next time

» changing our perspective by focusing on what rewards us and gives us pleasure, such as our family and friends.

Behaving with impartiality in *all* our interpersonal interactions can mean the difference between being accepted and listened to, or ignored. (As the boss you would probably prefer it wasn't the latter.)

CLARITY

Clarity of thinking and understanding keeps our brain in a place of safety. At work this depends a great deal on how clear we are with the messages we communicate. Clarity provides certainty, and the brain likes familiarity and recognisable patterns. In an uncertain world, this can be difficult, but we can look to achieve it by removing ambiguity and being transparent about the intention of our messages.

If the traffic is snarled up or a flight delayed, being kept informed helps us to know what to expect. It's the same with memos and workplace announcements: sharing the relevant information allays fear. A powerful negative emotion, fear can easily send us into a rapid downward spiral unless the brakes are put on quickly through the provision of clarity and certainty.

Effective communicators recognise the importance of:

» being really clear on the message conveyed

» providing as much information as possible so the message is complete

» being transparent about the true meaning of the message

» repeating the message several times

» inviting discussion about the message.

The media and social commentators are expert at producing a provocative headline or screen grab to seize our attention without providing any detail. Sparking our interest to read a news bulletin or watch a TV program, headlines and on-screen announcements are hooks to draw us in. To make an important decision, however, we need to have the confidence we are being given access to all the relevant facts.

EMPATHY

If you're wondering why empathy needs to be regarded as a leadership quality, consider this: empathy and trust together form the basis for all successful relationships, and business is all about relationships.

Empathy is good for our health and wellbeing. It enhances tolerance and reduces self-interest.

We commonly sense and mirror the emotions of others. Have you ever noticed how two people speaking together will mirror each other's behaviour, from crossing their legs to clasping their hands behind their heads? This *chameleon effect* demonstrates commonality: 'I get what you're saying'.

When we observe someone, say, picking up a cup of coffee, the mirror neurons in our brain fire off in the same way they would fire if we were doing it ourselves. This helps us to respond appropriately and extrapolate meaning from the cues available to us.

Being empathetic is not about being soft and pliant; it is a genuine reflection of understanding what someone might be experiencing or thinking. An empathetic leader will make hard decisions as needed, but from a place of humility and service. This softens the blow when announcing bad news and helps others remain resilient when coping with adversity.

Empathy matters to the bottom line because increasingly customers and staff expect greater personal recognition and satisfaction. Non-empathetic companies will find it harder to retain good staff who don't feel listened to or understood.

The caring professions have traditionally attracted those with naturally higher levels of empathy, but that doesn't mean empathy cannot not be learned. Indeed, some medical schools include empathy in their core curriculum. Telefonica Germany instituted an empathy training program that showed a 6 per cent increase in customer satisfaction in just six weeks.

A survey undertaken in 2015 in the UK identified LinkedIn, Microsoft and Audi as the top three empathetic companies based on the perspective of employees, customers and social media interactions. CEO Belinda Parmar from The Lady Geek summed up the new approach in a *Harvard Business Review* article aptly titled 'Corporate Empathy Is Not an Oxymoron'.

The human brain is particularly good at social affiliation. Having a boss or a manager who we feel cares about us has been shown to matter far more than how much we earn.

There are always going to be those times when we have to interact with people we don't get on with. When it is your boss, it can be fraught with problems. Being open about the fact that you have different perspectives can mitigate the negativity that would otherwise interfere with a working relationship.

Building empathy starts with showing consideration for others. It can involve an interaction as simple as holding open a door for someone, offering up your seat on the bus or listening to someone's complaint about being kept waiting. It can mean offering an unexpected compliment or thanking someone for contributing to a conversation or for working hard, which adds to their sense of community and belonging.

Incorporating the TRAICE elements into every conversation or interaction helps us to better understand not just ourselves but others too.

Each of the keys outlined in this introduction to high-performance thinking can assist us to get better results from everything we do. While the temptation is to jump in and fix or smarten up how we operate our brain, taking the time to ensure we have a firm foundation, beginning with a fit and healthy brain, makes it far easier to then polish up operational and interpersonal skills.

Remembering we are human first, acknowledging our faults, our biases and daily challenges, helps keep us grounded in what matters. Putting the humanity back into our lives and workplace starts with self-leadership. Although placed as the last key in the book, it is perhaps the one that matters most, because self-leadership means we can look forward to our future with confidence and clarity, and with the certainty that we can continue to adapt and thrive.

Conclusion

Cogito ergo sum.
René Descartes

The human brain is remarkable for its ability to adapt and evolve. The way we use our mental acuity to handle situations, stresses and sensory experiences that are unfamiliar to us is extraordinary.

The more we unravel the brain's secrets, the more we can marvel at its complexity and beauty.

Heading towards our future, it is reassuring to know we are in safe intellectual hands. We can rest assured our brain will maintain its phenomenal ability to evolve and adapt to meet the needs of a rapidly changing world.

Developing smarter sharper thinking is not hard, but it does require us to look after our brain in the right way. This involves conscious choice. Conscious choice in turn involves best thought practice. Best thought practice — that depends on having a healthy, fit brain.

If we are really serious about resolving the social challenges we currently face, such as rising levels of obesity, poor physical health, poor mental health and dementia, we need to stop and ask ourselves the hard questions. This is the first stage for working smarter not harder.

WHAT ISSUES DO I AS AN INDIVIDUAL NEED TO ADDRESS IN MY OWN LIFE? WHAT BEHAVIOURS DO I NEED TO STOP, START OR DO DIFFERENTLY?

To get the most out of our lives, to perform at our best, means starting from a foundational level. Creating a brain that is fit, healthy and optimised to work well begins with our choice of lifestyle.

It's not that we don't know what to do. Our brain knows what it needs. It got us this far, after all. We are already ahead on the evolutionary track (sorry dinosaurs).

What we have to do is think — and choose. *Think* to consciously implement those healthy choices that will make the biggest differences to our brain's performance. *Choose* to make our brain as healthy and fit as it can be.

MAKE A THOUGHTFUL CHOICE TO SAY YES TO A HIGH-PERFORMANCE BRAIN.

Being busy is no excuse. We are all busy. But often, it seems, we fall back on the excuse of being too busy rather than taking responsibility and being accountable for our own health and wellbeing.

In 2011 Barnes and Yaffe found that the number of people projected to develop Alzheimer's disease by 2050 could be halved if the top seven potentially modifiable risk factors were addressed. (This was based on the assumption of a causal link between each risk factor and Alzheimer's.)

Surely reducing our risk for cognitive decline has to be a no-brainer. (Yes, I groaned at that one too, sorry. Doctors may be intelligent, but we aren't necessarily good at being punny.)

The top seven risk factors are:

» low levels of education

» smoking

» inadequate physical activity

» depression

» midlife hypertension

» type 2 diabetes

» obesity.

As life expectancy increases, we expect to live longer with our physical and mental faculties intact. Undertaking activities to help achieve this quality of life is paramount.

An increasing proportion of people are now choosing to stay in the workplace beyond retirement age either because they enjoy their work and feel capable of continuing, or out of economic necessity. The retirement age is itself rising, which means more of us working into our eighth decade.

All these factors mean there will also be an increasing number of people diagnosed with some form of cognitive deficit who will need assistance to stay in the workplace for as long as possible.

Is your workplace geared up for this?

How we apply ourselves to our work on a daily basis is the second aspect of high-performance thinking and the future brain. Again, we are back to choices and best thought practice.

How do you schedule your day so as to focus on what matters when it matters? How do you remember what is relevant? How do you ensure you have the cognitive energy to solve problems and make the most appropriate decisions easily and quickly?

OUR CHOICE OF FOCUS CHANGES OUR BRAIN. OUR CHOICE OF THOUGHT DIRECTS OUR ACTIONS AND OUR OUTCOMES.

Factoring in those choices helps us to remain calm under pressure and maintain our energy; it motivates us to do our work and do it well.

The third aspect of smarter sharper thinking is to remind ourselves that whatever we do, and however we do it, it will in some way involve others. It's about being — and staying — human. Whether we are looking to become more creative, more collaborative or more influential as a leader, it's about developing and integrating our emotional and social intelligence.

Anthony Howard, author of *Humanise: Why Human-Centred Leadership Is the Key to the 21st Century,* believes we are facing a crisis in leadership and calls for a review of how we become the best we can be by re-examining our own moral compass and building a strong empathy for others.

Whatever foundation you choose to operate from, it will always include developing strong relationships. If you want to understand what is going on in someone else's head, you have to start with a greater awareness of self. If we are tuned in to what really motivates or drives us, it becomes easier to understand what motivates others and to see their perspective.

The 12 keys of *Smarter Sharper Thinking* provide an overview of what is possible. It's not a perfect or infallible system. We are not perfect beings. It's a framework that you can incorporate as an individual — as a human — when designing your own unique high-performance brain.

And, as someone who thinks smarter using conscious choice and clarity of thought you will know that what serves you well today will need to be upgraded again tomorrow. And that's the way it should be.

The impact of our technology — the human–computer interface — has not been addressed here. How do our genes, our environment and our technology interact to shape our thinking? That's the question to be addressed in the next book ...

Meanwhile I leave you with three questions and a thought, which is as it should be. First, the questions:

What do you need to start doing now to create a fitter, healthier brain?

What needs to change to allow you to operate at your personal best?

What will you do differently to introduce more meaning into your work and your relationships and increase your level of happiness and wellbeing?

As for that thought: René Descartes' famous quote with which this section began is usually translated as 'I think, therefore I am', but a more correct and useful rendering is:

I am thinking, therefore I exist.

With smarter sharper thinking, we can say:

I am smarter sharper thinking, therefore I excel.

Start excelling.

Sources

Introduction

Boedker, C, Vidgen, R, Meagher, K, Cogin, J et al. 2011. 'Leadership, Culture and Management Practices of High Performing Workplaces in Australia: The High Performing Workplaces Index.' Society for Knowledge Economics, Australian School of Business, UNSW.

The Centre for International Economics 2016. 'The Economic Value Of Pathology: Achieving Better Health, And A Better Use Of Health Resources.'

Diabetes Australia 2013, 'Diabetes in Australia', viewed 11 May 2015, www.diabetesaustralia.com.au/Understanding-Diabetes/Diabetes-in-Australia.

Direct Health Solutions 2017. '2017 Absence Management Survey Report.'

Ferrari, AJ, Charlson, FJ, Norman, RE., Patten SB. et al. 2013. 'Burden of depressive disorders by country, sex, age, and year: Findings from the Global Burden of Disease Study 2010', *PLOS Medicine*, vol. 10, no. 11, e1001547. Available from http://dx.doi.org/10.1371/journal.pmed.1001547 [11 May 2015].

Government Office for Science 2008, 'Mental capital and wellbeing: making the most of ourselves in the 21st century', viewed 11 May 2015, www.bis.gov.uk/foresight/our-work/projects/current-projects/mental-capital-and-wellbeing.

Lencioni, P 2012. *The Advantage: Why Organisational Health Trumps Everything Else in Business*, Jossey-Bass, New Jersey.

Medibank 2011. 'Sick at Work: The Cost of Presenteeism to Your Business and the Economy', report prepared as part the Medibank research series.

Professional Coaching And Mentoring Blog 2018. 'The Cost Of Sickies In Australia' http://www.exponentialprograms.com/professional/blog/tag/australian-sick-day-statistics/.

Nutrition

ABC Health and Wellbeing 2013. 'Caffeine - Health & Wellbeing', viewed 11 May 2015, http://www.abc.net.au/health/library/stories/2006/04/27/1829125.htm.

American Heart Association Meeting Report 2014. 'Trans Fat Consumption is Linked to Diminished Memory in Working-aged Adults', abstract 15572, 18 November.

Baumeister, Roy F & Tierney, John (2011). *Willpower: Rediscovering Our Greatest Strength*, Penguin, USA.

Borota, D, Murray, E, Keceli, G, Chang, A et al. 2014. 'Post-study caffeine administration enhances memory consolidation in humans', *Nature Neuroscience*, 17, pp. 201–3.

Katz, DL and Meller, S 2014. 'Can we say what diet is best for health?' *Annual Review of Public Health* 35, pp 83–103.

Krikorian, R, Shidler, MD, Nash, TA, Kalt, W et al. 2010. 'Blueberry supplementation improves memory in older adults', *Journal of Agricultural and Food Chemistry* vol. 58, no. 7, pp 3996–4000.

Lucas, M, Mirzaei, F, Pan, A, Okereke, OI et al. 2011. 'Coffee, caffeine, and risk of depression among women', *Archives of Internal Medicine*, vol. 171, no. 17, pp 1571–1578.

Ng, M, Gakidou, E et al. 2014. 'Global, regional, and national prevalence of overweight and obesity in children and adults during 1980–2013: A systematic analysis for the Global Burden of Disease Study 2013', *The Lancet*, vol. 384, no. 9945m pp. 766–781.

Sánchez-Villegas, A, Verberne, L, de Irala, J, Ruíz-Canela, M et al. 2011. 'Dietary fat intake and the risk of depression: The SUN Project', *PLOS ONE*, vol. 6, no. 1, e16268. Available from http://dx.doi.org/10.1371/journal.pone.0016268 [11 May 2015].

Scarmeus, N, Stern, Y, Tan, MX, Mayeux, R et al. 2006. 'Mediterranean diet and risk for Alzheimer's disease', *Annals of Neurology*, vol. 59, no. 6, pp. 912–21.

Singh-Manoux, A, Czernichow, S, Elbaz, A, Dugravot, A et al. 2012. 'Obesity phenotypes in midlife and cognition in early old age: The Whitehall II cohort study', *Neurology*, vol. 79, pp. 755–62.

Society for Neuroscience (SfN) 2012. 'This is your brain on food: Studies reveal how diet affects brain functions', *Science Daily*. viewed 11 May 2015, www.sciencedaily.com/releases/2012/10/121017091724.htm.

Society for the Study of Ingestive Behavior. 2014. 'Drinking sugar-sweetened beverages during adolescence impairs memory, animal study suggests'. *Science Daily*. viewed June 19 2015, www.sciencedaily.com/releases/2014/07/140729224906.htm.

Suominen-Taipale, AL, Partonen, T, Turunen, AW, Männistö, S et al. 2010. 'Fish consumption and omega-3 polyunsaturated fatty acids in relation to depressive episodes: A cross-sectional analysis', *PLOS ONE*, vol. 5, no. 5, e10530. Available from http://dx.doi.org/10.1371/journal.pone.0010530 [11 May 2015].

Tan, ZS., Harris, WS., Beiser, AS., Au, R et al. 2012. 'Red blood cell omega-3 fatty acid levels and markers of accelerated brain aging', *Neurology*, vol. 78, no. 9, pp. 658–664.

Thompson, JJ, Blair, MR & Henrey, AJ 2014. 'Over the hill at 24: Persistent age-related cognitive-motor decline in reaction times in an ecologically valid video game task begins in early adulthood', *PLOS ONE*, vol. 9, no. 4, e94215. Available from http://dx.doi.org/10.1371/journal.pone.0094215 [11 May 2015].

Tsivgoulis, G, Judd, S, Letter, AJ, Alexandrov, AV et al. 2013. 'Adherence to a Mediterranean diet and risk of incident cognitive impairment', *Neurology*, vol. 80, no. 18, 1684–1692.

Exercise

Baikler, K, Cutler, D & Song, Z 2010. 'Workplace wellness programs can generate savings', *Health Affairs*, vol. 29, no. 2, pp. 304–11.

Casey, L 2012. 'Stress and Wellbeing in Australia in 2012: A State-of-the-Nation Survey', Australian Psychological Society.

Centers for Disease Control and Prevention 2014. 'State Indicator Report on Physical Activity'. Atlanta, GA, US Department of Health and Human Services.

Chapman, SB, Aslan, S, Spence, JS, DeFina, LF. et al. 2013. 'Shorter term aerobic exercise improves brain, cognition, and cardiovascular fitness in aging', *Frontiers in Aging Neuroscience*, vol. 5, no. 75. Available from http://dx.doi.org/10.3389/fnagi.2013.00075 [11 May 2015].

Coulson, JC, McKenna, J & Field, M 2008. 'Exercising at work and self-reported work performance', *International Journal of Workplace Health Management*, vol. 1, no. 3, pp. 176–197.

Emery, CF, Hsiao, ET, Hill, SM & Frid, DJ 2003. 'Short-term effects of exercise and music on cognitive performance among participants in a cardiac rehabilitation program', *Heart Lung*, vol. 32, no. 6, pp. 368–373.

Katzmarzyk, P & Lee, IM 2012. 'Sedentary behaviour and life expectancy in the U.S: A cause related life table analysis', *BMJ Open*, vol. 2, no. 4, e000828. Available from http://dx.doi.org/10.1136/bmjopen-2012-000828 [11 May 2015].

Levine, JA, Vander Weg, MW, O'Hill, JO & Klesges, RC 2006. 'Non-exercise activity thermogenesis: The crouching tiger hidden dragon of societal weight gain', Arteriosclerosis, Thrombosis, and Vascular Biology, vol. 26, pp 729–736.

Lifestyle Statistics Team, Health and Social Care Information Centre 2014. 'Statistics on obesity, physical activity and diet: England'. Available from http://www.hscic.gov.uk/catalogue/PUB16988/obes-phys-acti-diet-eng-2015.pdf [11 May 2015].

Martin, K 2010. 'Brain Boost: Sport and Physical Activity Enhance Children's Learning', School of Population Health, University of Western Australia, prepared for the Department of Sport and Recreation, Government of Western Australia.

Ramazzini, B 2001. 'De morbis artificum diatriba [Diseases of workers]', *American Journal of Public Health*, vol. 91, no. 9, pp. 1380–1382.

Ratey, J, with Hagerman, E 2013. *Spark: The Revolutionary New Science of Exercise and the Brain*. New York, Little, Brown and Company.

Reynolds, G 2013. *The First Twenty Minutes: Surprising Science Reveals How We Can Exercise Better, Train Smarter, Live Longer*. New York, Penguin.

Rhodes, JS, Mustroph, ML, Chen, S, Desai, SC, Cay, EB et al. 2012. 'Aerobic exercise is the critical variable in an enriched environment that increases hippocampal neurogenesis and water maze learning in male C57BL/6J mice', *Neuroscience*, vol. 219, pp. 62–71.

Schatzkin, A, Matthews, CE, George, SM, Moore, SC et al. 2012. 'Amount of time spent in sedentary behaviours and cause-specific mortality in US adults', *American Journal of Clinical Nutrition*, vol. 95, no. 2, pp. 437–445.

Towers Watson 2014. 'Staying@Work™ Survey Report 2013/2014, United States'. Available from http://www.towerswatson.com/en/Insights/IC-Types/Survey-Research-Results/2013/12/stayingatwork-survey-report-2013-2014-us [11 May 2015].

Towers Watson 2014. 'The Path to Health and Productivity Effectiveness', Available from http://www.towerswatson.com/en/Insights/IC-Types/Ad-hoc-Point-of-View/2014/01/Towers-Watson-Health-Wellness-Seminar-Malaysia [11 May 2015].

Worksafe Victoria 2010. 'Healthy Workplace Kit: Your Guide to Implementing Health and Wellbeing Programs at Work'. Available from http://www.worksafe.vic.gov.au/wps/wcm/connect/f7093280439cdf6db37eb3145ee8dc5e/?a=17203 [11 May 2015].

Sleep

Faraut, B, Nakib, S, Drogou, C, Elbaz, M, et al. 2015. 'Napping reverses the salivary interleukin-6 and urinary norepinephrine changes induced by sleep restriction', *Journal of Clinical Endocrinology and Metabolism*, vol. 100, no. 3. e416-426. Available from http://dx.doi.org/10.1210/jc.2014-2566 [11 May 2015].

Frenda, SJ, Patihis, L, Loftus, EF, Lewis, HC, et al. 2014. 'Sleep deprivation and false memories', *Psychological Science*, vol. 25, no. 9, pp. 1674–1681.

Fryer, B 2006. 'Sleep deficit: The performance killer', *Harvard Business Review*, October.

Gillen, KA, Rosekind, MR, Graeber, RC, Dinges, DF, et al. 1994. 'Crew factors in flight operations IX: Effects of planned cockpit rest on crew performance and alertness in long-haul operations', *NASA Technical Memorandum*, 108839, NASA Ames Research Center, Moffett Field, CA.

Killgore, WD 2010. 'Effects of sleep deprivation on cognition', *Progress in Brain Research*, vol. 185, pp. 105–129.

Kott, J, Leach, G, & Yan, L 2012. 'Direction-dependent effects of chronic "jet-lag" on hippocampal neurogenesis', *Neuroscience Letters*, vol. 515, no. 2, pp. 177–180.

Kriegsfield, L, Gibson, EM, Wang, C, Tjho, S, et al. 2010. 'Experimental "jet lag" inhibits adult neurogenesis and produces long-term cognitive deficits in female hamsters', *PLOSONE*, vol. 5, no. 12, e15267. Available from http://dx.doi.org/doi:10.1371/journal.pone.0015267 [11 May 2015].

Morphy, H, Dunn, KM, Lewis, M, Boardman, HF, et al. 2007. 'Epidemiology of insomnia: A longitudinal study in a UK population', *Sleep*, vol. 30, no. 3, pp. 274–280.

Nedergaard, M, Xie, L, Kang, H, Xu, Q, et al. 2013. 'Sleep drives metabolite clearance from the adult brain', *Science*, vol. 342, no. 6156, pp. 373–377.

Rajaratnam, S, Howard, M & Grunstein, R 2013. 'Sleep loss and circadian disruption in shift work', *Medical Journal of Australia*, vol. 199, no. 8, pp 11–15.

Shapiro, CM, Williams, AJ. & Fenwick, PB, 2013. 'Alcohol and sleep I: Effects on normal sleep', *Alcoholism: Clinical & Experimental Research*, vol. 36, no. 4, pp. 539–549.

Sivertsen, B, Lallukka, T & Salo, P 2011. 'The economic burden of insomnia at the workplace: An opportunity and time for intervention?' *Sleep*, vol. 34, no. 9, pp. 1413–1425.

Sleep Health Foundation (2010). *Re-awakening Australia: The Economic Cost of Sleep Disorders in Australia*, report prepared by Deloitte Access Economics Pty Ltd. Available from http://www.sleephealthfoundation.org.au/more/research-news/88-re-awakening-the-nation.html [11 May 2015].

Vyazovskiy, VV, Olcese, U, Hanlon, EC, Nir, Y, et al. 2011. 'Local sleep in awake rats', *Nature*, vol. 472, pp. 443–447.

Wiseman, R 2014. *Night School: The Life-Changing Science of Sleep*. Pan Macmillan, London.

Mental stretch

Andraka, J 2013. A promising test for pancreatic cancer ... from a teenager, TED2013. Available from https://www.ted.com/talks/jack_andraka_a_promising_test_for_pancreatic_cancer_from_a_teenager [11 May 2015].

Capelli, G 2010. *Thinking Caps*, Capa Pty Ltd, Perth.

Fernandez, A, & Goldberg, E 2009. *The SharpBrains Guide to Brain Fitness: 18 Interviews with Scientists, Practical Advice, and Product Reviews, to Keep Your Brain Sharp*. SharpBrains Inc, USA.

Gruber, MJ, Gelman, BD, & Ranganath, C 2014. 'States of curiosity modulate hippocampus-dependent learning via the dopaminergic circuit', *Neuron*, vol. 84, no. 2, pp. 486–496.

Hsieh, LT, Gruber, MJ, Jenkins, LJ & Ranganath, C 2014. 'Hippocampal activity patterns carry information about objects in temporal context', *Neuron*, vol. 81, no. 5, pp. 1165–1178.

Melby-Lervag, M. and Hulme, C. (2012). 'Is working memory training effective? A meta-analytic review', *Developmental Psychology*, vol. 49, no. 2, pp. 270–291.

Sherwood, C, Gordon, AD, Allen, JS, Phillips, KA, et al. 2011. 'Aging of the cerebral cortex differs between humans and chimpanzees', *Proceedings of the National Academy of*

Sciences of the United States of America, vol. 108, no. 32, pp. 13029–13034.

Spencer-Smith, M. & Klingberg, T 2015. 'Benefits of a working memory training program for inattention in daily life: A systematic review and meta-analysis', *PLOS ONE*, vol. 10, no. 3, e0119522. Available from http://dx.doi.org/10.1371/journal.pone.0119522 [11 May 2015].

Taylor, JB 2009. *My Stroke of Insight: A Brain Scientist's Personal Journey*. Penguin, USA.

Focus

Bavelier, D 2012. *Your Brain on VideoGames*. TEDxCHUV. Available from http://www.ted.com/talks/daphne_bavelier_your_brain_on_video_games?language=en [11 May 2015].

Cook, P 2013. *The New Rules of Management: How to Revolutionise Productivity, Innovation and Engagement by Implementing Projects that Matter,* Wiley, Brisbane.

Evans, GW & Johnson, D 2000. 'Stress and open-office noise', *Journal of Applied Psychology*, vol. 85, no. 5, pp. 779–783.

Foroughi, C, Werner, NE, Nelson, ET & Boehm-Davis, DA 2014. 'Do interruptions affect quality of work?' *Human Factors*, vol. 56, no. 7, pp 1262–1271.

Fredrickson, B 2013. *Love 2.0: Finding Happiness and Health in Moments of Connection*, Plume, USA.

Goleman, D 2014. *Focus: The Hidden Driver of Excellence*, Bloomsbury, UK.

Hallowell, EM 2005. 'Overloaded circuits: Why smart people underperform', *Harvard Business Review*, January.

Jackson, M 2009. *Distracted: The Erosion of Attention and the Coming Dark Age*, Prometheus, New York.

Kleitman, N 1987. *Sleep and Wakefulness*, revised and enlarged edition, University of Chicago Press, Chicago.

Letvitin, D 2014. *The Organised Mind: Thinking Straight in the Age of Information Overload*, Dutton Penguin, USA.

Mark, G, Voida, S & Cardello, A 2012. 'A pace not dictated by electrons: An empirical study of work without email', in CHI '12 Proceedings of the SIGCHI Conference on Human Factors in Computing Systems, pp. 555–564. Available from ACM Portal: ACM Digital Library. [11 May 2015].

Pozen, RC 2012. *Extreme Productivity: Boost Your Productivity, Reduce Your Hours*. HarperBusiness, USA.

Rubinstein, J, Meyer, DE & Evans, JE 2001. 'Executive control of cognitive processes in task *switching*', *Journal of Experimental Psychology: Human Perception and Performance*, vol. 27, no. 4, pp. 763–797.

Schwartz, T 2010. *The Way We're Working Isn't Working: The Four Forgotten Needs That Energise Great Performance*. Free Press, New York.

Seppala, Emma 2017. 'What Is Your Phone Doing To Your Relationships?'. *Greater Good Magazine*, 2017. https://greatergood.berkeley.edu/article/item/what_is_your_phone_doing_to_your_relationships.

Turkle, S 2012. *Alone Together: Why We Expect More from Technology and Less from Each Other*. Basic Books, New York.

Wainwright, M 2005. 'E-mails "pose threat to IQ"', *Guardian Unlimited*, retrieved 2 May from www.guardian.co.uk.

Wang, Z, & Tchernev, JM 2012. 'The "myth" of media multitasking: Reciprocal dynamics of media multitasking, personal needs, and gratifications', *Journal of Communication*, vol. 62, no. 3, pp. 493–513.

Ward, Adrian F., Kristen Duke, Ayelet Gneezy, and Maarten W. Bos 2017. 'Brain Drain: The Mere Presence Of One'S Own Smartphone Reduces Available Cognitive Capacity', *Journal Of The Association For Consumer Research*, vol 2, no 2, pp. 140–154.

Watson, JM & Strayer, D 2010. 'Supertaskers: Profiles in extraordinary multitasking ability', *Psychonomic Bulletin & Review*, vol. 17, no. 4, pp. 479–485.

Mindset

Dweck, C 2007. *Mindset: The New Psychology of Success, How We Can Learn to Fulfil Our Potential*, Ballantine, New York.

Rosenthal, R & Jacobson, L 1968. *Pygmalion in the Classroom: Teacher Expectation and Pupils' Intellectual Development*, Holt, Rinehart & Winston, New York.

Healthy stress

Arnsten, AF 2009. 'Stress signalling pathways that impair prefrontal cortex structure and function', *Nature Reviews Neuroscience*, vol. 10, no. 6, pp. 410–422.

Davachi, L, Kiefer, T, Rock, D & Rock, L 2010. 'Learning that lasts through AGES', *Neuroleadership Journal*, vol. 3.

Festinger, L. and Carlsmith, JM 1959. 'Cognitive consequences of forced compliance', *Journal of Abnormal and Social Psychology*, vol. 58, no. 2, pp. 203–210.

Gordon, E, Barnett, KJ, Cooper, NJ, Tran, N, et al. 2008. 'An "Integrative Neuroscience" platform: Application to profiles of negativity and positivity bias', *Journal of Integrative Neuroscience*, vol. 7, no. 3, pp. 345–366.

Lieberman, MD, Eisenberger, NI, Crockett, MJ, Tom, SM, et al. 2007. 'Putting feelings into words: Affect labeling disrupts amygdala activity in response to affective stimuli', *Psychological Science*, vol. 18, no. 5, pp. 421–428.

McGonigal, K 2013. 'How to make stress your friend', TEDGlobal 2013. Available from http://www.ted.com/talks/kelly_mcgonigal_how_to_make_stress_your_friend?language=en [11 May 2015].

Ochsner, KN, Bunge, SA, Gross, JJ & Gabrieli, JDE 2002. 'Rethinking feelings: An fMRI study of the cognitive regulation of emotion', *Journal of Cognitive Neuroscience*, vol. 14, no. 8, pp. 1215–1229.

Rosser Jr, JC, Lynch, PJ, Cuddihy, L, Gentile, DA, et al. 2007. 'The impact of video games on training surgeons in the 21st century', *Archives of Surgery*, vol. 142, no. 2, pp. 181–186.

Runde, C & Flanagan, T 2010. *Developing Your Conflict Competence: A Hands-on Guide for Leaders, Managers, Facilitators, and Teams*, Jossey-Bass, San Francisco.

Mindfulness

Carlson, LE, Beattie, TL, Giese-Davis, J, Faris, P, et al. 2015. 'Mindfulness-based cancer recovery and supportive-expressive therapy maintain telomere length relative to controls in distressed breast cancer survivors', *Cancer*, vol. 121, no. 3, pp. 476–484.

Davidson, R, MacCoon, DG, Sheridan, JF, Kalin, NH, et al. 2013. 'A comparison of mindfulness-based stress reduction and an active control in modulation of neurogenic inflammation', *Brain, Behavior, and Immunity*, vol. 27, no. 1, pp. 174–184.

Esch, T 2014. 'The neurobiology of meditation and mindfulness meditation: Neuroscientific approaches and philosophical implications', *Studies in Neuroscience, Consciousness and Spirituality*, vol. 2, pp. 153–173.

Farb, NAS, Segal, ZV, Mayberg, H, Bean, J, et al. 2007. 'Attending to the present: Mindfulness meditation reveals distinct neural modes of self-reference', *Social Cognitive & Affective Neuroscience*, vol. 2, no. 4, pp 313–322.

Goleman, D 2013. 'The focused leader', *Harvard Business Review*, December.

Greider, CW & Blackburn, EH 1989. 'A telomeric sequence in the RNA of *Tetrahymena* telomerase required for telomere repeat synthesis', *Nature*, vol. 337, pp. 331–337.

Hölzel, BK, Carmody, J, Vangel, M, Congleton, C, et al. 2011. 'Mindfulness practice leads to increases in regional brain gray matter density', *Psychiatry Research: Neuroimaging*, vol. 191, no. 1, pp. 36–43.

Honoré, C 2005. *In Praise of Slow: How a Worldwide Movement Is Challenging the Cult of Speed*, Orion, UK.

Killingsworth, M. & Gilbert, DT 2010. 'A wandering mind is an unhappy mind', *Science*, vol. 330, no. 6006, pp. 932.

Langer, EJ 1990. *Mindfulness*. Da Capo Press, Boston.

Langer, E, Russell, T & Eisenkraft, N 2009. 'Orchestral performance and the footprint of mindfulness', *Psychology of Music*, vol. 37, no. 2, pp. 125–36.

Tan, CM 2014. *Search Inside Yourself: The Unexpected Path to Achieving Success, Happiness (and World Peace)*, HarperOne, USA.

Thoreau, HD 1854. *Walden*, Princeton University Press, US.

Thoreau, HD 1849. *On the Duty of Civil Disobedience*, Wilder Publications, US.

Zeidan, F, Johnson, SK, Diamond, BJ, David, Z, et al. 2010. 'Mindfulness meditation improves cognition: Evidence of brief mental training', *Consciousness and Cognition*, vol. 19, no. 2, pp. 597–605.

Zinn, JK 1990. *Full Catastrophe Living: Using the Wisdom of Your Body and Mind to Face Stress, Pain and Illness*, Bantam, New York.

Change ability

Blackburn, S, Ryerson, S, Weiss, L, Wilson, S, et al. 2010. 'How do I implement complex change at scale?', *McKinsey Quarterly Insights*, McKinsey and Company.

Duhigg, C 2013. *The Power of Habit: Why We Do What We Do in Life and Business*. Random House, UK.

Goleman, D, Boyatzis, R & McKee, A 2001. 'Primal leadership: The hidden driver of great performance', *Harvard Business Review*, December.

Kotter, J 2012. 'Leading Change: Why Transformation Efforts Fail.' *Harvard Business Review*, November.

McFarland, W 2012. 'This is your brain on organisational change', *Harvard Business Review*, October.

Sinek, S 2011. *Start with Why: How Great Leaders Inspire Everyone to Take Action*. Penguin, New York.

Zappos 2015. 'About Zappos Culture', viewed 11 May 2015, http://about.zappos.com/our-unique-culture/zappos-core-values.

Innovation

Blanchette, DM, Ramocki, SP, O'del, JN & Casey, MS 2005. 'Aerobic exercise and cognitive creativity: Immediate and residual effects', *Creativity Research Journal*, vol. 17, no. 2, pp. 257–264.

Chandra, ML & Levitin, D 2013. 'The neurochemistry of music', *Trends in Cognitive Sciences*, vol. 17, no. 4, pp. 179–193.

Colzato, LS, Szapora, A, Pannekoek, JN, & Hommel, B 2013. 'The impact of physical exercise on convergent and divergent thinking', *Frontiers in Human Neuroscience*, vol. 7, no. 824. Available from http://dx.doi.org/doi:10.3389/fnhum.2013.00824 [11 May 2015].

Gruberger, M, Ben-Simon, E, Levkovitz, Y, Zangen, A, et al. 2011. 'Towards a neuroscience of mind-wandering', *Frontiers in Human Neuroscience*, vol. 5, no. 56. Available from dx.doi.org/10.3389/fnhum.2011.00056 [11 May 2015].

IBM 2010 Global CEO Study 2010. *Creativity Selected as the Most Crucial Factor for Future Success*, media release, IBM, Armonk, NY, 18 May.

Jung-Beeman, M, Collier, A & Kounios, J 2008. 'How insight happens: Learning from the brain', *Neuroleadership Journal*, vol. 1, pp. 20–25.

Jung-Beeman, M, Bowden, EM, Haberman, J, Frymiare, JL, et al. 2004. 'Neural activity when people solve verbal problems with insight', *PLOS Biology*, vol. 2, no. 4, pp. 500–510.

Kounios, J & Jung-Beeman, M 2015. *The Eureka Factor: Aha Moments, Creative Insight and the Brain*, Random House, New York.

Kraus, C, Ganger, S, Losak, J, Hahn, A, et al. 2014. 'Gray matter and intrinsic network changes in the posterior cingulate cortex after selective serotonin reuptake inhibitor intake', *Neuroimage*, vol. 84, pp. 236–244.

De Manzano, Ö, Cervenka, S, Karabanov, A, Farde, L, et al. 2010. 'Thinking outside a less intact box: Thalamic dopamine D2 receptor densities are negatively related to psychometric creativity in healthy individuals', *PLOS ONE*, vol. 5, no. 5, e10670. Available from http://dx.doi.org/10.1371/journal.pone.0010670 [11 May 2015].

McGilchrist, I 2010. *The Master and His Emissary: The Divided Brain and the Making of the Western World*, Yale University Press.

Nemeth, C, Personnaz, B, Personnaz, M & Goncalo, JA 2004. 'The liberating role of conflict in group creativity: A study in two countries', *European Journal of Social Psychology*, vol. 34, no. 4, pp. 365–374.

Oikkonen, J, Huang, Y, Onkamo, P, Ukkola-Vuoti, L, et al. 2014. 'A genome-wide linkage and association study of musical aptitude identifies loci containing genes related to inner ear development and neurocognitive functions', *Molecular Psychiatry*, vol. 20, pp. 275–282.

Ornstein, R 1998. *The Right Mind: Making Sense of the Hemispheres*, Harvest, USA.

Perkins, D 2000. *The Eureka Effect: The Art and Logic of Breakthrough Thinking*, Norton, New York.

Pink, D 2005. *A Whole New Mind: Why Right Brainers Will Rule Our Future*, Penguin, New York.

Robinson, K 2006. *How Schools Kill Creativity*, TED2006. Available from http://www.ted.com/talks/ken_robinson_says_schools_kill_creativity [11 May 2015].

Ukkola-Vuoti, L, Kanduri, C, Oikkonen, J, Buck, G, et al. 2013. 'Genome-wide copy number variation analysis in extended families and unrelated individuals characterized for musical aptitude and creativity in music', *PLOS ONE*, vol. 8, no. 2, e56356. Available from http://dx.doi.org/10.1371/journal.pone.0056356 [11 May 2011].

Wills, TW, Soraci, SA, Chechile, RA & Taylor, HA 2000. ' "Aha" effects in the generation of pictures', *Memory and Cognition*, vol. 28, pp. 939–948.

Collaboration

Bear, JB & Woolley, AW 2011. 'The role of gender in team collaboration and performance', *Interdisciplinary Science Reviews*, vol. 36, no. 2, pp. 146–153.

Cacioppo, J & Patrick, W 2009. *Loneliness: Human Nature and the Need for Social Connection*. Norton, New York.

Capra, F 1997. *The Web of Life: A New Scientific Understanding of Living Systems*, Anchor, New York.

Dunbar, R, Lycett, J & Barrett, L 2005. *Evolutionary Psychology*, Oneworld Publications, UK.

Fox, J 2014. *The Game Changer: How to Use the Science of Motivation with the Power of Game Design to Shift Behaviour, Shape Culture and Make Clever Happen*, Wiley, Brisbane.

Garner, J 2014. *From Me to We: Why Commercial Collaboration Will Futureproof Business, Leaders and Personal Success*, Wiley, Brisbane.

Gensler 2008. '2008 Workplace Survey: United States', *Gensler Design+Performance Report*. Available from www.gensler.com/uploads/documents/2008_Gensler_Workplace_Survey_US_09_30_2009.pdf [11 May 2015].

Gensler 2016. 'The Gensler 2016 Workplace Survey Reveals Workplace Secrets Of The Most Creative And Innovative Companies', www.gensler.com/news/press-releases/us-workplace-survey-2016-findings.

Gensler 2016. 'U.S. Workplace Survey 2016 | Research & Insight | Gensler' viewed 05 October 2018, www.gensler.com/research-insight/workplace-surveys/us/2016.

Hart, D & Sussman, RW 2005. *Man the Hunted: Primates, Predators, and Human Evolution*, Westview, USA.

Lehrer, J 2012. 'GroupThink: The brainstorming myth', *The New Yorker*, 30 January.

Lieberman, MD 2013. *Social: Why Our Brains Are Wired to Connect*, Crown, New York.

Liebermann, M & Eisenberger, N 2009. 'Pains and pleasures of social life', *Science*, vol. 323, no. 5916, pp. 890–891.

Malone, T 2004. *The Future of Work: How the New Order of Business Will Shape Your Organization, Your Management Style and Your Life*, Harvard Business School Press, USA.

Social Science Bites 2013. 'Robin Dunbar on Dunbar Numbers' viewed 11 May 2015, www.socialsciencespace.com/2013/11/robin-dunbar-on-dunbar-numbers.

Surowieki, J 2005. *The Wisdom of Crowds: Why the Many Are Smarter Than the Few and How Collective Wisdom Shapes Business Economies, Societies and Nations*, Anchor, USA.

Warneken, F & Tomasello, M 2006. 'Altruistic helping in human infants and young chimpanzees', *Science*, vol. 311, pp. 1301–1303.

Woolley, AW & Malone, T 2011. 'Defend your research: What makes a team smarter? More women', *Harvard Business Review*, June.

Woolley, AW, Chabris, CF, Pentland, A, Hashmi, N, et al. 2010. 'Evidence for a collective intelligence factor in the performance of human groups', *Science*, vol. 330, no. 6004, pp. 686–688.

Zak, P 2013. *The Moral Molecule: How Trust Works*, Penguin, New York.

Leadership

Ariely, D 2012. What makes us feel good about our work?, TEDxRiodelaPlata. Available from http://www.ted.com/talks/dan_ariely_what_makes_us_feel_good_about_our_work [11 May 2011].

iOpenener Institute for People and Performance 2012. 'Job fulfillment, not pay, retains Generation Y talent'. Available from https://www.iopenerinstitute.com/media/73185/ iopener_institute_gen_y_report.pdf [11 May 2015].

Marmot, MG, Smith, GD, Stansfeld, S, Patel, C, et al. 1991. 'Health inequalities among British civil servants: The Whitehall II study', *The Lancet*, vol. 337, no. 8754, pp. 1387–1393.

Nelson, B 2012. *1501 Ways to Reward Employees*. Workman, New York.

Oswald, AJ, Proto, E, Sgroi, D 2015. 'Happiness and productivity'. *Journal of Labor Economics*, vol 33, iss 4, pp. 789–822.

Parmer, B 2015. 'Corporate Empathy Is Not an Oxymoron', *Harvard Business Review*, January.

Tabibnia, G & Lieberman, MD 2007. 'Fairness and cooperation are rewarding: Evidence from social cognitive neuroscience', *Annals of the New York Academy of Sciences*, vol. 1118, pp. 90–101.

Ulrich, D & Ulrich, W 2010. *The Why of Work: How Great Leaders Build Abundant Organisations that Win*, McGraw-Hill, USA.

Zenger, J & Folkman, J 2015. 'You have to be fast to be seen as a great leader', *Harvard Business Review*, February.

Conclusion

Barnes, DE & Yaffe, K 2011. 'The projected effect of risk factor reduction on Alzheimer's disease prevalence', *Lancet Neurology*, vol. 10, no. 9, pp. 819–828.

Gardner, H 2009. *Five Minds for the Future*, Harvard Business Press, USA.

Howard, A 2015. *Humanise: Why Human-Centred Leadership Is the Key to the 21st Century*, Wiley, Brisbane.